LEARN
french
in a Hurry

GRASP
THE BASICS OF
français
TOUT de SUITE!

Laura K. Lawless

Adams Media
Avon, Massachusetts

Copyright ©2007, F+W Publications, Inc.
All rights reserved. This book, or parts thereof, may not be reproduced in any
form without permission from the publisher; exceptions are made for brief
excerpts used in published reviews.

Published by
Adams Media, an F+W Publications Company
57 Littlefield Street, Avon, MA 02322. U.S.A.
www.adamsmedia.com

ISBN 10: 1-59869-289-5
ISBN 13: 978-1-59869-289-1

Printed in the United States of America.

J I H G F E D C B A

Library of Congress Cataloging-in-Publication Data
Lawless, Laura K.
Learn French in a hurry / Laura K. Lawless.
p.   cm.
ISBN-13: 978-1-59869-289-1 (pbk.)
ISBN-10: 1-59869-289-5 (pbk.)
1. French language—Textbooks for foreign
speakers—English. I. Title.
PC2129.E5L38 2007
448.2'421—dc22   2007016649

This publication is designed to provide accurate and authoritative information
with regard to the subject matter covered. It is sold with the understanding that
the publisher is not engaged in rendering legal, accounting, or other professional
advice. If legal advice or other expert assistance is required, the services of a
competent professional person should be sought.
    —From a *Declaration of Principles* jointly adopted by a Committee of the
American Bar Association and a Committee of Publishers and Associations

Many of the designations used by manufacturers and sellers to distinguish their
product are claimed as trademarks. Where those designations appear in this
book and Adams Media was aware of a trademark claim, the designations have
been printed with initial capital letters.

Contains portions of material adapted or abridged from *The Everything® Learning French Book*, by Bruce Sallee and David Hebert, Copyright ©2002, F+W
Publications, Inc.; *The Everything® French Grammar Book*, by Laura K. Lawless, Copyright ©2006, F+W Publications, Inc.; and *The Everything® French
Phrase Book* by Laura K. Lawless, Copyright ©2005, F+W Publications, Inc.

This book is available at quantity discounts for bulk purchases.
For information, please call 1-800-289-0963.

Contents

Introduction

BONJOUR! I'M so happy that you've decided to learn French. Learning French is a challenging but extremely rewarding task. Whether you are learning in order to travel to French-speaking countries, interact with native speakers in your community, or just learn more about the world we live in, being able to speak French will definitely come in handy. In addition to helping you communicate with more people, learning a new language can also teach you more about the cultures in which it is spoken.

French is the native language of millions of people in dozens of countries on five continents. It is often called the language of love and the language of culture, particularly fashion, art, ballet, and gastronomy. For many years it was also the language of diplomacy; in fact, French is one of the official or working languages of dozens of international organizations, including the United Nations, Interpol, and NAFTA.

Linguistically speaking, French is a Romance language, which means that it is descended from Latin and is related to Spanish, Italian, and Portuguese, so if you already speak one of those languages, you'll find it that much easier to learn French. On the other hand, French has also had a tremendous impact on English, as you will see by the number of similar words in the two languages.

Learning French takes effort, but the rewards are considerable. This book offers you an overview of French pronunciation concepts as well as the essential vocabulary and grammar that you need to master first. The most important thing to remember is that you need to practice—knowing all the verb conjugations won't do you any good if you don't put them to the test by talking or writing to other French speakers. So start studying, and then come practice with me at Learn French at About (*http://french.about.com*)!

01 / Beginning French

Learn Your ABCs and How to Pronounce Them

Where do you start when you want to learn French in a hurry? The alphabet, of course! While French and English use the same alphabet, in French, the letters are pronounced a little differently. If you ever have to spell your name out at a hotel, for example, you want to make sure that you're understood.

The French Alphabet

Letter	Sound
a	ahh
b	bay
c	say
d	day
e	euh
f	eff
g	jhay
h	ahsh
i	ee
j	jhee

The French Alphabet (continued)

Letter	Sound
k	kahh
l	ehll
m	ehmm
n	ehnn
o	ohh
p	pay
q	koo
r	aihr
s	ess
t	tay
u	ooh
v	vay
w	doo-bluh-vay
x	eeks
y	ee-grek
z	zed

Sounds

Most of the consonants in French are pronounced the same as in English, but many of the vowel sounds differ. It is almost impossible to describe the true sound of French using text. For best results, try to listen to actual French being spoken; only then can you appreciate the sound of the language.

Liaison, Elision, and Enchaînement

Some pronunciation areas are governed by the grammatical concepts elision and liaison, and *enchaînement* also affects pronunciation of certain words. Keep the following pronunciation points in mind. Liaison occurs when one word ends in a consonant that is normally silent and the following word begins with a vowel or mute *h*. It is only a concern in spoken French, of course, but it is still a part of the formal language rules. For example, you would pronounce *un enfant* as *uhn-nahn-fahn* ("a child"). When a pronoun that ends in a consonant is used with a verb that begins with a vowel, liaison occurs. *Nous avons*, for example, which means "we have," is pronounced *noo-za-vohn*, even though *nous* above has no *s* or *z* sound.

Elision occurs when two vowels or a vowel and mute *h* appear together—one at the end of a word, and the other at the beginning of the word immediately following it. The vowel at the end of the first word is replaced with an apostrophe. Consider the French word for water is *l'eau*, pronounced *low*. This is an example of an elision of *la + eau*.

Enchaînement, unlike elision, is a matter of pronunciation only; it does not affect written French. It does, however, operate in a similar fashion, pushing the sounds of words together. Instead of being governed by vowels and consonants, though, enchaînement is governed by phonetic sounds. And instead of affecting the last letter of a word, *enchaînement* affects the last sound. Consider the French equivalent to "she is," *elle est*. It is pronounced *eh-lay*.

Numbers and Counting

Okay, so now you know the alphabet and how to pronounce the letters, but what about numbers? Well, you are lucky once again! In addition to using the same alphabet as English, French uses the same numerical symbols. When the numbers are pronounced, however, there are striking differences.

There are actually two kinds of numbers. There are cardinal numbers, which are the regular numbers "one," "two," three," and so on. But there are also ordinal numbers, which define the relationship of the number to others, such as "first," "second," and "third."

Cardinal Numbers

Numbers from zero to nineteen are fairly straightforward:

▶ From Zero to Ten

French	Pronunciation	English
zero	zay-ro	zero
un(e)	uhn/oon	one
deux	deuh	two
trois	trwah	three
cinq	sank	five
six	sees	six
sept	set	seven
huit	wheat	eight
neuf	neuhf	nine
dix	dees	ten

▶ The Teens

French	Pronuniciation	English
onze	ohnz	eleven
douze	dooz	twelve
treize	trayz	thirteen
quatorze	ka-torz	fourteen
quinze	kayhnz	fifteen
seize	sayz	sixteen
dix-sept	dee-set	seventeen
dix-huit	dee-zweet	eighteen
dix-neuf	deez-noof	nineteen

The numbers twenty through sixty-nine follow a consistent pattern, very similar to the English way of naming a group of tens—like "twenty"—and following it with another word, such as "one," to form "twenty-one." In written French, the numbers are combined with a hyphen, with the exception of *et un*, which is two words and translates as "and one."

▶ **Numbers between 20 and 29**

French	Pronunciation	English
vingt	vehn	twenty
vingt et un	vehn-tay-uhn	twenty-one
vingt-deux	vehn-doo	twenty-two
vingt-trois	vehn-trah	twenty-three
vingt-quatre	vehn-kat-ruh	twenty-four
vingt-cinq	vehn-sank	twenty-five
vingt-six	vehn-sees	twenty-six
vingt-sept	vehn-set	twenty-seven
vingt-huit	vehn-wheet	twenty-eight
vingt-neuf	vehn-noof	twenty-nine

To form numbers between thirty and ninety-nine, simply add the appropriate number after the end of the word for the group of tens.

▶ **Numbers between 30 and 99**

French	Pronunciation	English
trente	trahnt	thirty
quarante	ka-rahnt	forty
cinquante	sank-ahnt	fifty
soixante	swahs-ahnt	sixty
soixante-dix	swahs-ahnt-dees	seventy
quatre-vingt	katr-vehn	eighty
quatre-vingt-dix	katr-vehn-dees	ninety

If you want to keep counting, the next number is *cent*. At 100, everything starts all over again.

▶ 100 and Counting

French	Pronunciation	English
cent	sahn	one hundred
cent trente-deux	sahn-trahnt-doo	one hundred and thirty-two
cent quatre-vingt-dix-neuf	sahn-katr-vehn-dees-noof	one hundred and ninety-nine

To indicate more than one hundred, the appropriate word is inserted before *cent*. English does the same thing; the only difference between "one hundred" and "two hundred" is the number at the beginning of it. When the number is an even hundred, *cent* is used in the plural—it has an *s* on the end to show that more than one is being indicated. The *s* is not pronounced, but it is important to remember for written French.

▶ Numbers from 200 to 1,000

French	Pronunciation	English
deux cents	doo-sahn	two hundred
quatre cents	katr-sahn	four hundred
neuf cents	noof-sahn	nine hundred

One thousand follows the same pattern as one hundred, using the word *mille*. Dates also fall into this category, when referring to a year.

▶ Numbers from 1,000 to 2 million

French	Pronunciation	English
mille	meel	one thousand

▶ Numbers from 1,000 to 2 million (continued)

French	Pronunciation	English
mille neuf cent quatre-vingt-dix	mee-yh noof sahn katr vehn dees	nineteen ninety
deux mille	doo mee-yh	two thousand
cent mille	sahn mee-yh	one hundred thousand
un million	uhn mee-yohn	one million
deux million	doo mee-yohn	two million

Ordinal Numbers

Related to cardinal numbers are ordinal numbers, which are used show a relationship between things or to indicate where a word happens to fit in a series. English examples are "first," "second," and "third." In French, the word for "first" is the only ordinal number that must agree in gender and number with the noun it modifies.

▶ The Ordinal First

Gender	Singular	Plural	Pronunciation
Masculine	premier	premiers	pruh-mee-yay
Feminine	première	premières	pruh-mee-air

The rest of the ordinal numbers don't change to agree with gender, but still add an *s* to agree with a plural noun.

▶ Ordinal Numbers

French	Pronunciation	English
deuxième	duh-zee-ehmm	second
troisième	twah-zee-ehmm	third
quatrième	ka-tree-ehmm	fourth
cinquième	sank-ee-ehmm	fifth
sixième	see-zee-ehmm	sixth

> ▶ **Ordinal Numbers (continued)**

septième	set-ee-ehmm	seventh
huitième	whee-tee-ehmm	eighth
neuvième	noo-vee-ehmm	ninth
dixième	dee-zee-ehmm	tenth
la troisième fois	la twah-zee-ehmm fwa	the third time

Ordinal numbers in French are formed using the cardinal number; this is very similar to the way English modifies numbers by adding "th" to the end of the cardinal number.

To form an ordinal a number in French, simply drop the *-e* from the end of the cardinal number and add *-ième* to the end. If the cardinal number does not end in *e*, simply add the *-ième* ending to the word. This works for all numbers but these three: *premier*, which is unique when compared to the other ordinal numbers; *cinquième*, which adds a *u* after the *q*; and *neuvième*, which changes the *f* into a *v*.

In English, you commonly see ordinal numbers like "first" and "second" abbreviated in writing as "1st" and "2nd." French does this too, but the small characters following the Arabic numerals are different. The number one is followed by a small *er* when it is abbreviated in the masculine, and a small *re* when abbreviated in the feminine. All others are followed by a small *e*.

> ▶ **Ordinal Numbers Abbreviations**

French	Pronunciation	Abbreviations	English
premier (m)	pruh-mee-yay	1er	first
première (f)	pruh-mee-aihr	1re	first
deuxième	doo-zee-ehm	2e	second
dix-huitième	dee-zwee-tee-ehm	18e	eighteenth

To Begin Your Vocab Lesson, True Cognates

One of the main components of language learning is vocabulary—memorizing the thousands of words that you need to talk about the world around you. For English speakers, one of the nice things about learning French is that there are some shortcuts you can take when learning vocabulary. For example, there are hundreds of true cognates—words that look similar in the two languages and have the same or similar meanings. These are nearly always nouns or adjectives. For example, the English word "accident" and the French word meaning the same thing, *un accident*, look and sound the similar. Keep your eye out for these cognates throughout your studies because they will help you learn vocabulary, but don't be fooled! Although words may look and sound alike, they may have different meanings. Always check a dictionary or ask a native speaker before assuming that similar words mean the same thing.

Don't Be Tricked! False Cognates

Although the preceding section can be very helpful when you are studying vocab, don't let it lull you into a false sense of security. Not all words that look alike mean the same thing—there are also hundreds of false cognates: words that look alike but have different meanings. There are also many semi-false cognates; that is, words that have several meanings, only some of which are similar in the two languages. The following table of some of the most common false and semi-false cognates will give you a good starting point for some serious work with a dictionary.

▶ Common False and Semi-False Cognates

French Word	English Word	French Meaning
assister	assist	attend
collège	college	junior high school
crayon	crayon	pencil
déception	deception	disappointment
demander	demand	to ask, to request
entrée	entrée	appetizer
gros	gross	big
librairie	library	bookstore
pièce	piece	room, coin
sale	sale	dirty
zone	zone	slum; area

Remember, the words in the table above do not mean the same thing! There are hundreds of false cognates and there are hundreds of true cognates. The bottom line is that you just need to be careful—if a French word looks a lot like an English one, it might mean the same thing, but it might not. Look it up in the dictionary just to be on the safe side!

02 / Building Your Vocabulary

Days and Dates

Let's face it, you've got to be able to tell what day it is. And this is a case in which you just have to learn some new vocabulary in order to get by—little words, like days of the week and months of the year.

▶ Days of the Week

French	Pronunciation	English
lundi	luhn-dee	Monday
mardi	mahr-dee	Tuesday
mercredi	mair-cruh-dee	Wednesday
jeudi	jeuh-dee	Thursday
vendredi	vahn-druh-dee	Friday
samedi	sahm-dee	Saturday
dimanche	dee-mahnsh	Sunday

▶ Months of the Year

French	Pronunciation	English
janvier	jahn-vee-ay	January
février	fayv-ree-ay	February
mars	mahrs	March
avril	ah-vreehl	April
mai	may	May
juin	jwehn	June
juillet	jwee-ay	July
août	ah-oot	August
septembre	sep-tahm-br	September
octobre	ok-tob-br	October
novembre	noh-vehm-br	November
décembre	day-sehm-br	December

In written French, days of the week and months of the year are not capitalized, unless they happen to be used at the beginning of a sentence.

Telling Time

French doesn't have words for "a.m." and "p.m." Time is usually expressed on a 24-hour clock. Thus 3 p.m. is translated as *quinze heures* or *15h*.

- Quelle heure est-il? Il est… (What time is it? It's…)
- Keh leur ay teel; ee lay…
- une heure (one o'clock)
- deux heures (two o'clock)
- trois heures trente/et demie (3:30)
- cinq heures moins le quart (4:45)
- midi (noon)
- minuit (midnight)

Words You Need to Know

The following vocabulary list includes a few basic words you can quickly master. They're fairly easy to remember, and you'll probably find yourself using them extensively whenever you speak French.

▶ **Basic French Words**

French	Pronunciation	English
oui	whee	yes
non	nohn	no
excusez-moi	ek-scoo-zay-mwah	excuse me
s'il vous plait	seel-voo-play	please
merci	mair-see	thank you
merci beaucoup	mair-see bow-coo	thank you very much
Pardon?	pahr-dohn	Pardon me?
Monsieur	meu-syoor	Mr.
Madame	mah-dahm	Mrs.
Mademoiselle	mahd-mwah-zel	Miss

Salutations and Greetings

The following vocabulary list includes words and expressions that you can use as simple greetings or responses to address friends and family.

▶ **Common Expressions**

French	Pronunciation	English
bonjour	bohn-jhoor	hello, good morning, good afternoon
adieu	ah-dyuh	farewell
au revoir	oh-rhe-vwahr	good bye
à vos souhaits	ah-vo soo-eh	bless you (after someone sneezes)
bienvenue	bee-ehn-veh-noo	welcome

▶ Common Expressions (continued)

bonne chance!	buhnn-shahnce	good luck!
bonne nuit	buhnn-nwee	good night, sleep well
bonsoir	bohn-swahr	good evening
bravo	brah-vo	well done
de rien	de-ree-en	you're welcome
merci	mehr-see	thank you
merci beaucoup	mehr-see boh-koo	thank you very much
Salut!	sah-loo	Hi! Bye!
Santé!	sahn-tay	Cheers!

Family, Friends, and You!

Family

The following vocabulary list includes French terms for common familial relationships. These words are all nouns, can appear as the subject or object of the sentence, and follow the same rules as the nouns.

▶ Your Family

French	Pronunciation	English
le cousin	le koo-zehn	cousin
la cousine	la koo-zeen	cousin
la femme	la fehm	wife
la famille	la fah-mee	family
la fille	la fee	daughter
le fils	le fees	son
le frère	le frehr	brother
la grand-mère	la grahn-mehr	grandmother
le grand-père	le grahn-pehr	grandfather
les grand-parents (m)	les grahn-pahr-anh	grandparents
le mari	le mahr-ee	husband
la mère	la mehr	mother

la nièce	la nee-ess	niece
le neveu	le ne-vuh	nephew
un oncle	uh-nonkl	uncle
les parents (m)	lay pahr-ahn	parents
le père	le pehr	father
la sœur	la soor	sister
la tante	la tahnt	taunt
la belle-mère	la bell-mehr	stepmother
le beau-père	le bo-pehr	stepfather
la demi-sœur	la deu-mee-soohr	half-sister
le demi-frère	le deu-mee-frehr	half-brother

Holidays and Occasions

The following vocabulary list includes some special occasions and holidays that you probably spend celebrating with friends or family. These expressions can stand on their own as simple expressions, or you can use them as part of other sentences.

▶ **Greetings and Sayings**

French	Pronunciation	English
bon anniversaire	boh-nah-nee-vehr-sehr	Happy Birthday
bonne année	buhnn ah-nay	Happy New Year
felicitations	fay-lee-see-ta-syohn	Congratulations
Joyeux Noël	jhwoy-oo no-ell	Merry Christmas
Joyeuses Pâques	jwoy-ooz pahck	Happy Easter
meilleurs vœux	may-euhr vuh	Best Wishes

Friends

The following vocabulary list includes some common French terms for friends.

▶ Who's Who?

French	Pronunciation	English
un(e) ami(e)	uh-nah-mee	friend
le copain (m)	le ko-pahn	friend, pal, boyfriend
la copine (f)	la ko-peen	friend, pal, girlfriend
le petit ami	le p-tee-tah-mee	boyfriend
la petite amie	la p-teet-ah-mee	girlfriend
le/(la) voisin(e)	le vwah-zehn	neighbor

Pets

To many people, pets can be like members of the family, so what better place to learn some words for different kinds of pets? The following list includes some common household pets. If you have a pet, be sure to memorize the word for him or her in French!

▶ Pet Names

French	Pronunciation	English
un animal	uh-nah-nee-mal	pet
un chat	uhn sha	cat
un chien	uhn shee-ehn	dog
un poisson	uhn pwa-ssohn	fish
un hamster	uhn-ahm-ster	hamster
un oiseau	uh-nwa-zo	bird

Parts of the Body

The following vocabulary list contains some French terms for parts of the body.

▶ Body Parts

French	Pronunciation	English
les cheveux (m)	lay shuh-vuh	hair
le corps	le kohr	body
la tête	la tett	head

▶ Body Parts (continued)

French	Pronunciation	English
le visage	le vee-zahj	face
un œil	ooh-nooy	eye
les yeux (m)	lay zyeu	eyes
le nez	le nay	nose
la joue	la jhoo	cheek
la bouche	la boosh	mouth
une oreille	ooh-nohr-ay	ear
le cou	le koo	neck
la poitrine	la pwah-treen	chest
un estomac	uh-nay-sto-mahk	stomach
le bras	le brah	arm
le dos	le doh	back
la jambe	la jham	leg
le genou	le jhen-oo	knee
la cheville	la sheh-veey	ankle
le pied	le pee-eh	foot

When referring to parts of the body in French, you don't use a possessive adjective like you do in English. In English we say things like "my hand" or "my arm," but in French, a reflexive verb is used instead:

- Je me brosse les dents. (I am brushing my teeth.)
- Je me lave les mains. (I am washing my hands.)

If translated literally, these sentences say something like "I brush the teeth of myself," so you can't translate literally.

Clothing
The following vocabulary list contains a number of French terms for clothing and other things you can buy in a shop, including men's and women's clothes.

▶ Everyday Clothing Items

French	Pronunciation	English
le manteau	le mahn-toh	coat
le pardessus	le pahr-dess-oo	overcoat
un imperméable	uh-nahm-pehr-may-ahblh	raincoat
la veste	la vest	jacket
le blouson	le bloo-zohn	jacket
le complet veston	le cohm-pleht veh-stohn	suit
le maillot	le my-oh	bathing suit
un uniforme	uh-noo-nee-form	uniform
le pantaloon	le pahn-tah-loon	pants, trousers
le jean	le jheen	jeans
le pyjama	le pee-jhah-mah	pajamas
la chemise	la shuh-meez	shirt
les chaussettes (f)	lay shoh-set	socks

Colors of the Rainbow

The following vocabulary list contains some French adjectives for colors. As adjectives, when used with a noun, they must agree in number and in gender.

▶ Colors

Masculine	Feminine	English
noir (nwahr)	noire (nwahr)	black
bleu (bleuh)	bleue (bleuh)	blue
marron (mahr-ohn)	marron (mahr-ahn)	brown
vert (vehr)	verte (vehrt)	green
gris (gree)	grise (greez)	grey
orange (ohr-ahnjh)	orange (ohr-ahnj)	orange
rose (rhoze)	rose (rhoze)	pink
violet (vee-oh-lay)	violette (vee-oh-lett)	purple
rouge (rhoojh)	rouge (rhoojh)	red
blanc (blahnk)	blanche (blahnsh)	white
jaune (jhown)	jaune (jhown)	yellow

Describing Things and People

You can use a number of different phrases to refer to things and people, depending on the situation. This section describes the various constructions you can use.

Il est

In English, we often use the phrase "it is" to describe things: it is blue, it is old, it is hot. In French, this can be done using *il est* or *c'est*. Both forms can mean the same thing, ranging from "he is," "she is," or "it is," depending on the construction of the sentence. Each form, however, is used at a different time.

Il est is the correct choice in the following circumstances. If the subject of the sentence is female, then you use *elle est* to make it agree.

Using a Single Adjective

When using a single adjective that refers to a specific person or a specific thing, *il est* is the proper construction. The adjective will agree in gender and number with the subject of the sentence. You can also use it in other tenses instead of just in the present.

- Je connais cet homme. Il est intelligent.
  (I know that man. He is intelligent.)
- J'aime ce jardin. Il est bien.
  (I love this garden. It is nice.)

Referring to a Profession

When simply stating that a person is of a certain profession, the phrase *il est* or *elle est* is used, and the noun appears with no article.

- Elle est médecin. (She is a doctor.)
- Il est pharmacien. (He is a pharmacist.)

Referring to Nationalities

When stating that a person is of a certain nationality, *il est* or *elle est* is used with the adjective, without an article.

- Elle est française. (She is French.)
- Il est anglais. (He is English.)

Referring to Religious Beliefs

When you wish to state that a person is of a certain religious belief or denomination, *il est* or *elle est* is used with an adjective, which also appears without an article, like the previous constructions.

- Elle est catholique. (She is Catholic.)
- Il est protestant. (He is Protestant.)

C'est

The phrase *c'est* also means "it is," but it is used in different circumstances from *il est*. It is a contraction of ce and est, and therefore doesn't actually use a subject pronoun.

With a Proper Name

When you wish refer to someone using his or her proper name, *c'est* is the appropriate choice.

- C'est Yvon Dumont. (It's Yvon Dumont.)
- C'est Michel. (It's Michael.)

With a Disjunctive Pronoun

When you want to say things like "it is me," *c'est* is the proper construction.

- C'est moi. (It is me.)
- C'est elle. (It is her.)

When Referring to a Situation or Idea

C'est is often used with a singular masculine adjective to refer to states of being or ideas.

- Oui, c'est vrai. (Yes, that's right.)
- J'acheterai le livre, c'est certain.
  (I will buy the book, it's certain.)

When Referring to a Noun That Is Modified by Other Words

When a noun is used with adjectives that modify or refine the meaning of the noun, *c'est* is the appropriate choice. Even a single article used with a noun is enough to modify it and make it necessary to use the *c'est* construction.

- C'est un livre excellent. (It's an excellent book.)
- C'est une pomme. (It's an apple.)

Il y a

In English, we often use phrases like "there is" and "there are" to refer to the general existence of things. In French, this is done with the phrase *il y a*. The French word *y* is an object pronoun. In this construction, it is the rough equivalent of the English "there." Even when *il y a* is used with a plural or feminine object, the subject and verb don't change. This is a French idiomatic expression that does not translate literally.

■ Il y a un bon film au cinéma.
   (There is a good film at the theatre.)
■ Il y a une grande vedette en ville.
   (There is a big star in town.)

You can also use the construction *il y a* as a question to ask if something exists. You could use the phrase *est-ce que* in front of it to form the question, or you can use inversion. When inversion is used, however, the pronoun retains its regular position in front of the verb, so you must insert a *t* in between.

■ Y a-t-il un bon film ici? (Is there a good film here?)
■ Y a-t-il une femme ici? (Is there a lady present?)

Voilà
Voilà is used to indicate something specific. It is actually a preposition that means "there is," "there are," or even "that is." *Voilà* takes the place of both the subject and the verb, being used only with the object of the sentence.

■ Voilà les enfants. (There are the children.)
■ Voilà une fenêtre. (There is a window.)

Because *voilà* doesn't really use a verb, you don't have to worry about agreement with any of the words; articles must still agree with the nouns, however.

Your Daily Routine
The following vocabulary list includes a number of French terms for activities you sometimes find yourself doing throughout the day.

▶ Morning Routine

French	Pronunciation	English
bâiller	by-yay	to yawn
faire sa toilette	fehr sa twah-lett	to wash up
faire son lit	fehr son lee	to make the bed
aller travailler	ah-lay trav-eye-ay	to go to work

▶ Evening Routine

French	Pronunciation	English
se reposer	se rhe-poe-zay	to have a rest
faire la sieste	fehr la see-est	to have a nap
se déshabiller	se day-sahb-ee-ay	to get undressed
mettre son réveil	met-ruh son ray-vay	to set the alarm clock

Coming and Going

Sometimes it's fun just to wander aimlessly and discover all kinds of hidden treasures. If you're in a hurry, though, there's no shame in asking for directions.

- Where is…? It's…
- Où se trouve…? C'est…
- oo seu troov; say

▶ Directions

French	Pronunciation	English
à gauche	ah gosh	left
à droite	ah drah	right
tout droit	too draw	straight (ahead)
à côté de	ah ko tay deu	next to
en haut/en bas	an ho, an ba	up/down
nord	nohr	north
sud	sood	south
est	ehst	east
ouest	oo west	west

Modes of Transportation

The following vocabulary list includes a number of French words associated with travel and methods of transportation.

▶ **Types of Transportation**

French	Pronunciation	English
la voiture	la vwah-toor	car
le taxi	le tak-see	taxi
le camion	le kah-mee-ohn	truck
un autobus	u-naut-oh-boos	bus
le métro	le may-troh	subway
un avion	u-nah-vee-ohn	plane

▶ **Tour Destinations**

French	Pronunciation	English
le restaurant	le rehs-toh-rahn	restaurant
le musée	le moo-zay	museum
la banque	la bahnk	bank
une église	ooh-nay-gleez	church
le cinéma	le si-nay-mah	movie theater
le théâtre	le tay-ahtruh	theater
la poste	la pohst	post office
le parc	le parhk	park
un hôpital	u-noh-pee-tahl	hospital

Money

Because money is always an issue when traveling, the following vocabulary list includes some common French terms related to money and banking.

▶ Money Terms

French	Pronunciation	English
de l'argent (m)	de lahr-jhahn	money
de l'argent liquide (m)	de lahr-jhahn lee-keed	cash
la pièce	la pee-ess	coin
le portefeuille	le pohrt-fooy	wallet
la banque	la bahnk	bank
le taux de change	le toh de shahnhj	exchange rate

In a Restaurant

The following vocabulary list includes a number of French words you may come across in a restaurant. Don't forget to peruse the beverage section, also in this chapter.

▶ Restaurant Terms

French	Pronunciation	English
le restaurant	le rhes-tohr-ahn	restaurant
le serveur	le sehr-veuhr	waiter
la serveuse	la sehr-veuz	waitress
l'addition (f)	lah-diss-yohn	check, bill
le pourboire	le poohr-bwahr	tip
les hors d'œuvre (m)	lay ohr-duhv	appetizer
la soupe	la soop	soup
la salade	la sah-lahd	salad
le plat principal	le plah prihn-see-pahl	main course
le dessert	le deh-sehr	dessert

Beverages

The following list contains a number of French terms for things you can drink—memorize your favorites.

▶ Drink Terms

French	Pronunciation	English
le café	le ka-fay	coffee
le café au lait	le ka-fay oh lay	coffee with milk
la camomille	la ka-mho-mee	chamomile tea
le chocolat chaud	le shok-oh-la show	hot chocolate
le thé	le tay	tea
l'eau (f)	low	water
l'eau minérale (f)	low mih-nay-rahl	mineral water
le lait	le lay	milk
le lait écrémé	le lay ay-kree-may	skim milk
le jus de fruit	le jhu de frwee	fruit juice
l'alcool (m)	lahl-kuhl	alcohol
la bière	la bee-aihr	beer
le vin rouge	le vehn rhooj	red wine
le vin blanc	le vehn blahnk	white wine

The following vocabulary list contains a number of French verbs and expressions related to shopping.

▶ Shopping Vocabulary

French	Pronunciation	English
acheter	ahsh-tay	to buy
choisir	shwa-zeer	to choose
coûter	koo-tay	to cost
dépenser	day-pahn-say	to spend
échanger	ay-shahn-jhay	to exchange
payer	pay-ay	to pay
vendre	vahn-druh	to sell

That last table got you interested? Confused perhaps? Read on and learn how to use these verbs to put it all together and make sentences!

03 / Grammar

Intro to French Grammar

This is where languages get tricky. Concepts, rules, and exceptions. Let's break it down and start from the beginning. French is a Romance language, although that's not why it's called the language of love. In linguistic terms, "Romance" comes from the word Roman and simply means "from Latin." The complete language family classification of French is Indo-European > Italic > Romance. Here are some things to know about the language classification of French:

- Indo-European is the largest language family and contains most European, American, and Asian languages, including Latin, Greek, Gaelic, Polish, and Hindi.
- Italic basically refers to Latin.
- Romance languages are originally from Western Europe, although due to colonization, some of them are found all over the world. French, Spanish, Italian, and Portuguese are all Romance languages.

Since Romance languages are all descended from Latin, they tend to be similar in many ways. If you have already studied another Romance language, you will find that some French concepts are very easy for you because you already learned about them when studying a previous language.

Blueprint of a Sentence

As strange as it may seem, learning a foreign language like French will help you grasp certain English grammar rules as well. Let's look at the structure of a sentence. Each sentence can be broken down into two parts: subject and predicate. The subject is the word or phrase that does the action and carries the description. The predicate does the rest; it is the action.

> *Consider the following in English:*
> subject. . . predicate
> My friends and I . . . go to the movies.
> The girl that I had seen last Friday. . . isn't home today.
> We. . . like it.

Note that the subject answers the question "who or what?" and the predicate answers what the subjects is or does. English and French sentences can be broken down similarly. Let's look at each part separately.

Parts of Speech

Subjects and predicates can be futher broken down into parts of speech. The term "part of speech" refers to the grammatical classification of the function or purpose of a word. All words can be categorized into one of nine parts of speech: nouns, articles, adjectives, pronouns, verbs, adverbs, prepositions, conjunctions, and interjections.

Nouns

French nouns and articles are two separate but interdependent parts of speech. A noun is a word that represents a thing, either concrete (e.g., a chair, a doctor) or abstract (e.g., life, love). Traditionally a noun is defined as a "person, place, or thing," but that description is sometimes considered too limiting and, therefore, "idea" and/or "quality" are sometimes added to the definition.

The most important thing to know about French nouns is that each one has a gender—either masculine or feminine. It is very important to learn a French noun's gender along with the noun itself because articles, adjectives, and some verbs have to agree with nouns; that is, they change according to the gender of the noun they modify. The best way to learn the gender of nouns is to make your vocabulary lists with the definite or indefinite article. That is, instead of making a list like this:

▶ **Noun Gender**

French	English
homme	man
femme	woman
garçon	boy
fille	girl

You should make your list like this, so that you learn the gender along with the word:

▶ **Noun**   **Gender**
French   *English*

un homme	man
une femme	woman
un garçon	boy
une fille	girl

In other words, the gender is part of the word. Think of the French word for "man" not as *homme* but rather as *homme* (m) or (*un*) *homme*.

Gender and Number of Nouns

One of the characteristics of nouns is that they may have up to four forms, depending on their gender and number. There are up to four possible forms for each noun: masculine singular (waiter, *serveur*), feminine singular (waitress, *serveuse*), masculine plural (waiters, *serveurs*), and feminine plural (waitresses, *serveuses*).

Articles

An article is the part of speech used in front of a noun to indicate the noun's application: whether it is specific, nonspecific, or partial. The three kinds of French article—definite, indefinite, and partitive—must agree in gender and number with the nouns they modify.

The French definite article corresponds to "the" in English. There are four forms of the French definite article: *le, la, l'*, and *les*. Which definite article to use depends on three things: the noun's gender, number, and first letter.

▶ **Singular Articles**

Masculine	*Feminine*	*Before Vowel or Mute H*
le	la	l'
le garçon	la fille	l'ami, l'homme

▶ Plural Articles

Masculine	Feminine	Before Vowel or Mute H
les	les	les
les garçons	les filles	les amis, les homes

The definite article has two main uses: to indicate a specific noun and to indicate the general sense of a noun.

Indefinite Articles

The singular French indefinite article corresponds to "a," "an," or "one" in English. The plural corresponds to "some." There are three forms of the French indefinite article: *un, une*, and *des*. The indefinite article usually refers to a nonspecific person or thing. In a negative construction, the indefinite article changes to *de*, meaning "not any."

▶ Indefinite Singular Articles

Masculine	Feminine
un	une
un garçon	une fille
un ami	une amie

▶ Indefinite Plural Articles

Masculine	Feminine
des	des
des garçons	des filles
des amis	des amies

Indefinite Uses

- J'ai vu un homme. (I saw a man.)
- Il veut des pommes. (He wants some apples.)

"Not Any"

- J'ai des stylos. (I have some pens.)
- Je n'ai pas de stylos. (I don't have any pens.)

Partitive Articles

The French partitive article corresponds to "some" or "any" in English. There are four forms of the French partitive article: *du, de la, de l'*, and *des*. Note that, like the definite article, the partitive article has four forms, and the one to use depends on three things: the noun's gender, number, and first letter. If the noun is plural, use *des*. If it's singular starting with a vowel or mute *h*, use *de l'*. If it's singular and starts with a consonant or aspirated *h* (nonmute h), use *du* if it's masculine and *de la* if it's feminine.

▶ **Singular Examples**

Masculine	Feminine	Before Vowel or Mute H
du	de la	de l'
du pain	de la glace	de l'eau
du thé	de la bière	de l'huile

▶ **Plural Examples**

Masculine	Feminine	Before Vowel or Mute H
des	des	des
des pois	des asperges	des haricots

The partitive article indicates an unknown or un-specified quantity of something, usually food or drink. It is often omitted in English.

- Veux-tu du thé? (Do you want [some] tea?)
- J'ai mangé de la salade hier. (I ate [some] salad yesterday.)

Like the indefinite article, the partitive article changes to *de*, meaning "not any," in a negative construction.

- Je n'ai mangé de soupe. (I didn't eat any soup.)
- Je ne veux pas de thé. (I don't want any tea.)

Adjectives

Adjectives are words that modify (describe) nouns. Adjectives can qualify, specify, or limit the nouns they modify and can describe shape, color, size, and many other aspects of nouns. First, in English, adjectives are always found in front of the noun, but most French adjectives are placed after it. Second, French adjectives change to agree in gender and number with the nouns that they modify.

- Demonstrative adjectives indicate which specific noun is being talked about (*ce livre*—this book)
- Exclamative adjectives express a strong sentiment such as admiration about a noun *(quel livre!*—what a book!)
- Indefinite adjectives modify nouns in an unspecific sense (*chaque livre*—each book)
- Interrogative adjectives ask for information about a noun (*quel livre?*—which book?)
- Negative adjectives negate a noun (*aucun livre*—no book)
- Possessive adjectives indicate the owner of a noun (*mon livre*—my book)

Like articles, French adjectives have to agree in gender and number with the nouns that they modify, which means that there can be up to four forms of each adjective. The rules for making the majority of adjectives feminine and plural are very similar to those for nouns. Most adjectives add *e* for feminine and *s* for plural.

Position of Adjectives

The position of adjectives can be a problem for learners of French because the type and meaning of the adjective dictate whether it should be placed before or after the noun. This concept can be frustrating, but with patience and practice it will eventually become second nature.

After the Noun

Descriptive adjectives are usually placed after the noun they modify, particularly when they have an analytical meaning.

- du café noir (black coffee)
- un homme français (a French man)

Before the Noun

A small number of adjectives are placed before the noun, and the acronym "BANGS" can help you memorize most of them:

Beauty
Age
Number
Good and bad
Size

These adjectives, as well as a few others, precede the noun because they are considered inherent qualities. Examples of these types of adjectives follow.

- une jolie fleur (pretty flower)
- un jeune enfant (young child)

Pronouns

Pronouns are the part of speech that allows you to avoid repeating yourself. Pronouns substitute for nouns. They can save you time when speaking French and allow your language to sound more natural. There are many different kinds of pronouns, which are divided into two categories: personal and impersonal.

There are six possible combinations of "number" and "person" that let you know who or what is performing or receiving the action of a verb. There are two numbers (singular and plural) and three persons (first, second, and third), making a total of six grammatical persons, each of which has at least one of each type of personal pronoun.

▶ **Personal Pronouns**

Person	Singlular	Plural
First	I	we
Second	you	you
Third	he, she, it, one	they

Personal pronouns change according to the grammatical person that they represent. There are five types of French personal pronouns:

- Subject
- Stressed
- Direct object
- Indirect object
- Reflexive

▶ Subject Pronoun Forms

English	French
1st person	
I	je
we	nous
2nd person	
you	tu/vous
you	vous
3rd person masculine	
he, it	il
they	ils
3rd person feminine	
she, it	elle
they	elles
3rd person nonspecific	
one	on

▶ Stressed Pronoun Forms

English	French
1st person	
me	moi
us	nous
2nd person	
you	toi
you	vous
3rd person masculine	
him	lui
them	eux
3rd person feminine	
her	elle
them	elles
3rd person nonspecific	
oneself	soi

Stressed pronouns are used in the following ways: to emphasize nouns or pronouns, when a sentence has more than one subject, in response to questions, and after prepositions.

Direct Object Pronouns

The direct object is the person or thing that receives the action of the verb in a sentence. To find the direct object in a sentence, ask the question Who? or What? (*Qui?* or *Quoi* ?)

▪ Il voit Marie. (He sees Marie)
▪ [Who does he see? Marie.]

Both French and English have direct object pronouns which replace the direct object. This is so that we don't say things like "Marie was at the bank today. When I saw Marie I smiled." It's much more natural to say "Marie was at the bank today. When I saw her I smiled."

There is at least one direct object pronoun for each grammatical person.

▶ Direct Object Pronouns

French	English	French	English
me/m'/ moi	me	nous	us
te/t'	you	vous	you
le/l'	him, it (masc)	les	them
la/l'	her, it (fem)		

In English, direct object pronouns follow the verb, but in French they precede the verb.

Indirect Object Pronouns

Indirect objects differ from direct objects, which receive the action of the verb in the sentence. Indirect objects are the people or things in a sentence to/for whom/what the action of the verb occurs. They are often preceded by a preposition.

- Je parle à Marie. (I'm talking to Marie.)
- [*To whom* am I talking? To Marie.]

Indirect object pronouns replace the indirect object. The French indirect object pronouns are:

▶ Indirect Object Pronouns

French	English	French	English
me/m'/moi	me	nous	us
te/t'	you	vous	you
lui	him, her, it	leur	them

French indirect object pronouns, like direct object pronouns, must precede the verb.

Demonstartive Pronouns

Demonstrative pronouns essentially replace a demonstrative adjective + a noun. Therefore, like demonstrative adjectives, demonstrative pronouns can refer to something nearby or far away. That is, *celui* and *celle* can mean "this one" or "that one," and *ceux* and *celles* can mean "these" or "those."

▶ Demonstrative Pronouns

Gender	Singular	Plural
Masculine	celui	ceux
Feminine	celle	celles

Demonstrative pronouns must be used in one of three types of constructions:

1. With the suffixes *-ci* or *-là* (see demonstrative adjectives) in order to distinguish between this one/these and that one/those.

▨ Quelle fille l'a fait, celle-ci ou celle-là?
▨ (Which girl did it, this one or that one?)

2. With a preposition, usually de, to indicate possession or origin.

▨ Quel film veux-tu voir? Celui de la France ou celui du Canada?
▨ (Which movie do you want to see? The one from France or the one from Canada?)

3. With a relative pronoun + dependent clause.

▨ Celui qui a menti sera puni.
▨ (He who/Whoever lied will be punished.)

Indefinite Pronouns
French indefinite pronouns, sometimes called affirmative indefinite pronouns, are nonspecific. They can be the subject of a sentence, the object of a verb, or the object of a preposition.

▨ Je veux te montrer quelque chose.
  (I want to show you something.)
▨ Tout le monde est prêt. (Everyone is ready.)

▶ Indefinite Pronouns

French	English
un(e) autre	another one
d'autres	others
certain(e)s	certain ones
chacun(e)	each one
plusieurs	several
quelque chose	something
quelqu'un	someone
quelques-uns	some, a few
tout	everything
tout le monde	everyone

Prepositions

A preposition is a word or phrase used to indicate a relationship between a verb, adjective, or noun that precedes the preposition and a noun that follows the preposition. Some English prepositions are: about, above, to, below, with, before, after, around, at, and for. The French prepositions can be divided into categories including prepositions dealing with time and place, as well as those that are paired with verbs.

- Je parle à David. (I'm talking to David.)
- Il est de Montréal. (He is from Montreal.)

▶ Most Common Prepositions

French	English
à	to, at, in
après	after
avant	before
avec	with
chez	at the home/office of
dans	in

▶ Most Common Prepositions (continued)

French	English
de	from, of, about
en	in, on, to
pour	for
sans	without
sur	on
vers	toward

Geographical Prepositions

Because French prepositions do not always parallel English prepositions in terms of meaning and usage, and because French nouns are gendered, knowing which French preposition to use with countries, cities, and other geographical names can be somewhat confusing. Often you simply have to memorize the following rules.

▶ Countries and Continents

Masculine	Feminine	Plural
au Maroc	en France	aux Fidji
à l'Iran	en Espagne	aux USA
du Maroc	de France	des Fidji
de l'Iran	d'Espagne	des USA

▶ States and Provinces

Masculine	Feminine
dans le Texas	en Louisiane
en Ohio	en Alberta
du Manitoba, d'Illinois	de Virginie, de Géorgie

▶ Cities and Islands

City	Singular Island	Plural Islands
J'habite à Londres.	Je vais à Hawaï.	Je vais aux Fidji.
Je suis de Rome.	Je suis de Malte.	Je suis des Maldives.

Adverbs

An adverb is an invariable word that modifies a verb, an adjective, or another adverb. Adverbs provide details like when, how, where, how often, or to what degree something is done about the word they modify. There are many different types of adverbs.

▶ Adverbs of Frequency

French	*English*
encore	again
jamais	ever, never
rarement	rarely
souvent	often
toujours	always, still
quelquefois	sometimes
tous les jours (mois, etc.)	every day (month, etc.)
une (deux, trois) fois	once (twice, three times)

▶ Adverbs of Place

French	*English*
autour	around
derrière	behind
dessous	below
dessus	above
devant	in front
en bas	down(stairs)
en haut	up(stairs)
ici	here
là	there
n'importe où	anywhere
nulle part	nowhere
partout	everywhere

▶ Adverbs of Time

French	English
alors	then
après	after
aujourd'hui	today
avant	before
déjà	already, ever
demain	tomorrow
hier	yesterday
immédiatement	immediately
longtemps	for a long time
maintenant	now
n'importe quand	anytime
tout de suite	right away

Clauses

A clause is a group of words containing a subject and a verb. Although a clause contains a subject and a verb, a clause is not the same thing as a sentence. A sentence must contain at least one clause, but a clause is not necessarily a sentence by itself—it can be a sentence fragment. There are three different kinds of clauses.

1. An independent clause expresses a complete idea and stands alone. It is neither dependent upon nor the dependent of another clause.

- L'homme habite ici. (The man lives here.)
- J'ai dit la vérité. (I told the truth.)

2. A main clause expresses something that is modified by one or more subordinate clauses.

- J'ai dit *que tu avais tort*. (I said that you were wrong.)
- L'homme *dont je parle* habite ici. (The man that I'm talking about lives here.)

3. A subordinate or dependent clause does not express a complete idea and cannot stand alone: it is attached to a main clause by a subordinate conjunction or a relative pronoun. When introduced by a relative pronoun, it may be known as a relative clause.

- *J'ai dit* que tu avais tort. (I said that you were wrong.)
- *L'homme* dont je parle *habite ici*. (The man that I'm talking about lives here.)

Relative Pronouns

Relative pronouns link subordinate clauses to main clauses, and the most important French relative pronouns are *qui* and *que*. There are no standard translations for these words; depending on context, the English equivalent might be "who," "whom," "that," or "which." Note that in French, relative pronouns are required; in English, they are often optional.

Qui replaces the subject (person or thing) in the subordinate clause
- Je cherche l'étudiant. Il a perdu son sac à dos. > Je cherche l'étudiant qui a perdu son sac à dos.
- I'm looking for the student who lost his back-pack.

Qui also replaces an indirect object (person only) after a preposition.
- C'est l'homme avec qui j'habite.
- That's the man with whom I live. / That's the man I live with.

Que replaces the direct object (person or thing)

- J'ai acheté le livre. Mon frère l'aimait. > J'ai acheté le livre que mon frère aimait.
- I bought the book (that) my brother liked.

The third relative pronoun, lequel, replaces an indirect object that is not a person.

- Le livre dans lequel j'ai vu…
- The book in which I saw…

Indefinite Relative Pronouns

Indefinite relative pronouns are similar in usage to relative pronouns: they link subordinate/relative clauses to main clauses. The difference is that regular relative pronouns have a specific antecedent, and indefinite relative pronouns do not.

There are four common indefinite relative pronouns; each form is used only in a particular structure, as summarized in the following table.

▶ Indefinite Relative Pronouns

Usage	Pronoun	Meaning
Subject	ce qui	what
Direct object	ce que/qu'	what
Object of *de*	ce dont	which, what
Object of another preposition	quoi	which, what

Conjunctions

Conjunctions are words that are used to join parts of a sentence together. In English, common conjunctions are "and," "or," and "but." You can use the following French conjunctions in the same way as you use English ones:

▶ Common Conjunctions

French	English
donc	so, then, therefore
ensuite	next
et	and
ou	or
puis	then
mais	but

Two Types of Conjunction

There are two types of French conjunction: coordinating and subordinating. The difference between coordinating and subordinating conjunctions is very simple: coordinating conjunctions join two words or groups of words with an equal value; subordinating conjunction join a subordinate/dependent clause to a main clause.

1. Coordinating conjunctions join words and clauses.

- ▦ Il ne mange ni poulet ni poisson.
  (He eats neither chicken nor fish.)
- ▦ J'aime lire et écrire. (I like reading and writing.)

▶ Common Coodrinating Conjunctions

French	English
car	because (since)
donc	so
et	and
et…et	both…and
ou	or
ni…ni	neither…nor
mais	but

2. Subordinating conjunctions join dependent clauses to main clauses.

- J'ai dit que je suis américain.
  (I said that I am American.)
- Il est parti parce qu'il est en retard.
  (He left because he is late.)

▶ **Common Subordinating Conjunctions**

French	English
parce que	because
pendant que	while
pour que	so that
puisque	since, as
quand	when
que	that
sans que	without

Verbs

The verb is the action word in a sentence—the word that says what happens (I walk) or describes a state of being (I am happy). Verbs are one of the most essential parts of speech; they are a required element in every sentence.

Verb Forms: Establishing Number and Person

Number and person indicate the grammatical person—who or what is performing the action of the verb. Once again, there are six grammatical persons, and each has at least one subject pronoun.

▶ Grammatical "People"
French Subject Pronouns

je	nous
tu	vous
il/elle	ils/elles

Conjugating French Verbs

The basic form of a verb is called the infinitive and is considered the name of the verb. The English infinitive is "to" followed by a verb, while the French infinitive is a single word with one of three endings: *-er, -ir,* or *-re.*

Types of Verbs

There are four main types of French verbs: regular, stem-changing, irregular, and reflexive. Another way to divide up verbs is by their endings—all French verbs end in *-er, -ir,* or *-re.* For regular verbs, these endings are very important because they indicate which set of verb endings to use when conjugating those verbs. Most French verbs are regular, which means that once you know how to conjugate one regular *-er, -ir,* and *-re* verb, you can conjugate the majority of French verbs. Below are some examples to help you get started.

▶ -ER Verbs

French	*English*
aimer	to like or to love
chercher	to look for
détester	to hate
étudier	to study
parler	to talk, to speak
penser	to think
regarder	to watch, to look at
travailler	to work

| trouver | to find |
| visiter | to visit (a place) |

▶ -IR Verbs

French	*English*
agir	to act
avertir	to warn
choisir	to choose
établir	to establish
finir	to finish
nourrir	to feed, to nourish
obéir	to obey
punir	to punish
réussir	to succeed
vieillir	to grow old

▶ -RE Verbs

French	*English*
attendre	to wait (for)
défendre	to defend
descendre	to descend
entendre	to hear, to understand
perdre	to lose
prétendre	to claim
rendre	to give back, to return something
répondre	to answer
vendre	to sell

All French verbs have to be "conjugated" or "inflected," that is, changed according to how they are used. In most cases, French verbs are conjugated by removing the infinitive ending to find the "radical," or "stem," and then adding the ending appropriate to the grammatical person, tense, and mood. These endings are different for each tense and mood, which means that each verb has dozens of different forms. But don't get discouraged! There are patterns to the conjugations of most verbs. There are a total of five elements in conjugation: number, person (which you've already gotten through!) tense, mood, and voice.

Tense, Mood, and Voice

The three verb conjugation elements you need to understand are tense, mood, and voice. These three work together to explain when an action takes place, the attitude of the speaker toward the action, and the relationship between the subject and verb.

Making Sense of Tense

Tense refers to the time a verb's action takes place. The main tenses are present, past, and future, though there may be two or more verb tenses within those primary categories. For example, there are several French past tenses: simple past (preterite), compound past, imperfect, past perfect, and past anterior.

There are two kinds of tenses. A simple tense is a verb form that consists of a single word: *je mange* (I eat), *nous parlons* (we talk), *il étudiera* (he will study). A compound tense is a verb form made up of two words—an auxiliary verb plus past participle: *j'ai mangé* (I have eaten), *il aurait étudié* (he would have studied).

Get in the Mood

Mood refers to the attitude of the speaker toward the action/state of the verb—how likely or factual a statement is. The French language has three to six moods, depending on how you look at it. The three moods that everyone agrees on are indicative, subjunctive, and imperative; the conditional, infinitive, and participle may or may not be considered moods by different grammarians.

Indicative

The indicative is what you might call the "normal" mood—it indicates a fact: *J'aime lire* (I like to read), *Nous avons mangé* (We ate). The indicative is the most common mood and has the most tenses.

Subjunctive

The subjunctive expresses subjectivity, such as doubt and unlikelihood: *Je veux que tu le fasses* (I want you to do it), *Il est rare que Chantal sache la réponse* (It's rare for Chantal to know the answer). . It has present and past forms, but no future—the present tense is used for current as well as future actions. Note that the subjunctive is rare in English but common in French.

Imperative

The imperative gives a command: *Écris la lettre* (Write the letter), *Allons-y!* (Let's go!) The imperative is the only verb form that does not require a subject or subject pronoun—the conjugation of the verb lets you know who is expected to perform the action of the verb.

Conditional

The conditional describes a condition or possibility: *J'aimerais aider* (I would like to help), *Si tu venais avec nous, tu apprendrais beaucoup* (If you came with us, you would learn a lot). The conditional is considered a separate mood by most but a subcategory of the indicative by a few grammarians.

Infinitive

The infinitive is the name of the verb: *parler* (to speak), *finir* (to finish), *vendre* (to sell). The infinitive is used most commonly after another verb or as a noun; however, as the latter it is usually translated by a gerund (the *-ing* form of a verb in English): *je veux aller* (I want to go), *voir c'est croire* (seeing is believing).

Participle

The participle is the adjectival form of the verb and comes in two varieties. The present participle ends in *-ant* and is used mainly as a qualifier adjective: *parlant* (speaking), *finissant* (finishing). The past participle usually ends in *-é, -i,* or *-u* (for *-er, -ir,* and *-re* verbs, respectively) and is used mainly in compound tenses: *parlé* (spoke, spoken), *fini* (finished), *vendu* (sold).

Find Your Voice

Voice refers to the relationship between the subject and verb. There are three voices in French:

1. **Active voice**—the subject performs the action: *Je lave la voiture* (I'm washing the car).
2. **Passive voice**—the action is performed on the subject by an agent, which may be stated or implied: *La voiture est lavée* (The car is being washed), *Le livre a été vendu par Chantal* (The book was sold by Chantal).
3. **Reflexive voice**—the subject performs the action on itself: *Je me lave* (I'm washing myself).

Active voice is the most common voice in French, followed by reflexive voice, which is much more common in French than in English. More than in English, the passive voice is usually avoided in French.

Verb Forms, According to Tense and Mood

Once you know the tense and mood that you would like to use, you have a verb form and you can consider its conjugations. To get an idea about how tense and mood fit together in French, take a look at this list:

Indicative
Past: Preterite, imperfect, present perfect, pluperfect, past anterior
Present: Present indicative
Future: Future indicative, future perfect

Subjunctive
Past: Past subjunctive, imperfect subjunctive, pluperfect subjunctive (rarely used)
Present/future: Subjunctive

Imperative
Past: Past imperative
Present: Imperative

Conditional
Past: Past conditional
Present/future: Conditional

Participle
Past: Past participle
Present: Present participle

Infinitive
Present: Infinitive
Past: Past infinitive

Present Tense

The present tense (*le présent*) is the most common French tense. The French present tense is used in much the same way as the English present tense, with one major exception. In English, we have what is called "aspect," a grammatical term that indicates the relationship of the verb's action to the passage of time. The three aspects can be seen in these examples: "I eat," "I am eating," and "I do eat." French, however, does not have aspect—all of the above are translated by *je mange*.

If you want to emphasize the fact that something is happening right now, as you might with "I am eating," you can use *être en train de*: *Je suis en train de manger*—I am (in the process of) eating (right now).

Regular Verbs

Regular verbs are those that follow one of three sets of conjugation rules. Let's take a look at our three categories: regular *-er* verbs, regular *-ir* verbs, and regular *-re* verbs, each of which has its own set of conjugations.

-er Verbs

There are more *-er* verbs than any other type—they are among the most common and useful French verbs. To conjugate an *-er* verb in the present tense, remove the infinitive ending to find the radical and then add the appropriate *-er* endings, as follows:

▶ **Conjugating –er Verbs**

Pronoun	Ending	Pronoun	Ending
je	-e	nous	-ons
tu	-es	vous	-ez
il/elle	-e	ils/elles	-ent

Thus to conjugate *parler* (to talk, speak), you would remove the infinitive ending to find the radical *parl-* and then add these endings, for example:

▶ **Example: Conjugating Parler**

Noun	Ending	Noun	Ending
je	parle	nous	parlons
tu	parles	vous	parlez
il/elle	parle	ils/elles	parlent

Regular verbs that end in *-ier*, like *étudier* (to study), follow the same pattern: drop *-er* to find the stem *étudi-* and then add the endings. Just be careful to keep the *i*.

▶ **Ending with –ier, Example Etudier**

Noun	Ending	Noun	Ending
j'	étudie	nous	étudions
tu	étudies	vous	étudiez
il/elle	étudie	ils/elles	étudient

Remember that if the verb begins with a vowel or mute *h*, *je* changes to *j'*.

-IR Verbs

Regular *-ir* verbs are the second largest category of French verbs. To conjugate an *-ir* verb, remove the infinitive ending and then add the *-ir* endings, as follows:

▶ Conjugating –*ir* Verbs

Pronoun	Ending	Pronoun	Ending
je	-is	nous	-issons
tu	-is	vous	-issez
il/elle	-it	ils/elles	-issent

So to conjugate *choisir* (to choose) you would remove the infinitive ending to find the radical *chois-* and then add the appropriate endings:

▶ Example: Conjugating *Choisir*

Noun	Ending	Noun	Ending
je	choisis	nous	choisissons
tu	choisis	vous	choisissez
il/elle	choisit	ils/elles	choisissent

-RE Verbs

The smallest category of regular verbs end in -*re*. To conjugate an -*re* verb, remove the infinitive ending and then add the -*re* endings, as follows:

▶ Conjugating –*re* Verbs

Pronoun	Ending	Pronoun	Ending
je	-s	nous	-ons
tu	-s	vous	-ez
il/elle	-t	ils/elles	-ent

Thus to conjugate *descendre* (to go down, descend), you would remove the infinitive ending to find the radical *descend-* and then add the appropriate endings.

▶ **Example: Conjugating** *Descendre*

Pronoun	Ending	Pronoun	Ending
je	descends	nous	descendons
tu	descends	vous	descendez
il/elle	descend	ils/elles	descendent

Irregular Verbs

Unfortunately it's not always that simple. Without a doubt, you will come across verbs that don't seem to follow any of the rules. These are irregular verbs, those that have conjugations specific to just one or a handful of verbs. Here are a few groups of irregular verbs that share conjugations.

Irregular -ir Verbs

There are two groups of irregular *-ir* verbs. The first group includes the verbs *dormir, mentir, partir, sentir, servir, sortir*, and their derivations (e.g., *repartir, endormir*). All of these verbs take the following endings:

▶ **Conjugating Irregular** *–ir* **Verbs**

Pronoun	Ending	Pronoun	Ending
je	-s	nous	-ons
tu	-s	vous	-ez
il/elle	-	ils/elles	-ent

The second group of irregular *-ir* verbs includes *couvrir, cueillir, offrir, ouvrir, souffrir*, and their derivations. The interesting thing about these verbs is that they end in *-ir* but are conjugated exactly like regular *-er* verbs, so the endings are:

▶ Conjugating Irregular –*ir* Verbs

Pronoun	Ending	Pronoun	Ending
je	-e	nous	-ons
tu	-es	vous	-ez
il/elle	-e	ils/elles	-ent

Irregular -re Verbs

There are three types of irregular -*re* verb; the first group includes *rompre* (to break) and its derivatives. The endings for these verbs are as follows:

▶ Conjugating Irregular –*re* Verbs

Pronoun	Ending	Pronoun	Ending
je	-s	nous	-ons
tu	-s	vous	-ez
il/elle	-t	ils/elles	-ent

The second group of irregular -*re* verbs includes *prendre* (to take) and all of its derivatives. The endings for these verbs are the same as for regular -*re* verbs:

▶ Conjugating Irregular –*re* Verbs

Pronoun	Ending	Pronoun	Ending
je	-s	nous	-ons
tu	-s	vous	-ez
il/elle	-	ils/elles	-ent

The third group of irregular -*re* verbs includes *battre, mettre*, and all of their derivatives. The endings for these verbs are again the same as for regular -*re* verbs; however, these verbs drop the second *t* in the stem of the singular forms. It is easier to learn how to conjugate this verb if you see it as an example of something. Take a look at the conjugated verb of *battre*:

▶ **Conjugating Irregular −re Verbs**

Pronoun	Ending	Pronoun	Ending
je	bats	nous	battons
tu	bats	vous	battez
il/elle	bat	ils/elles	battent

Reflexive Verbs

Reflexive verbs are organized according to their regular/irregular/stem-changing verb classification, but have an additional characteristic: they are preceded by a reflexive pronoun which indicates that the subject is performing the action of the verb upon itself (*je me lave*—I'm washing myself) or that multiple subjects are performing a reciprocal action (*ils s'écrivent*—they are writing to each other).

Reflexive verbs must be conjugated according to their infinitive ending and regular/stem-changing/irregular status, and also preceded by the appropriate reflexive pronoun. For example:

▶ **Example: *Se Laver* (to wash oneself)**

Pronoun	Ending	Pronoun	Ending
je	me lave	nous	nouslavons
tu	te laves	vous	vouslavez
il/elle	se lave	ils/elles	selavent

Reflexive pronouns are a type of personal pronoun used only with pronominal verbs (in the reflexive voice). Pronominal verbs are those which indicate that the subject is performing the action of the verb upon him/her/itself.

Reflexive pronouns change to agree with the subject of the sentence. The reflexive pronoun is placed directly in front of the verb in all tenses except the imperative.

▶ Reflexive Pronouns

Noun	Pronoun	Noun	Pronoun
je	me / m	nous	nous
tu	te / t'	vous	vous
il/elle	se / s	ils/elles	se / s

Here are some examples of conjugated reflexive verbs with reflexive pronouns:

- Je me lève. (I'm getting up.)
- Nous nous parlons. (We're talking to each other.)

Irregular Verbs That You Must Know!

The conjugations you learned will allow you to conjugate hundreds of regular verbs. However, sometimes you just have to memorize the irregular ones. Here, you'll learn how to conjugate and use ten of the most useful irregular French verbs.

Aller—To Go

The French verb *aller* means "to go," and can be used to express most of the English actions associated with "to go."

- Je vais à Paris. (I'm going to Paris.)
- Il va avec vous. (He's going with you.)
- Vas-tu au cinéma? (Are you going to the movies?)
- Ça va bien. (It's going well.)

▶ Present Tense of *Aller*

Noun	Ending	Noun	Ending
je	vais	nous	allons
tu	vas	vous	allez
il/elle	va	ils/elles	vont

Avoir—To Have

Avoir means "to have" in most of the same ways that this verb is used in English, including having in one's possession and currently experiencing.

- J'ai un crayon. (I have a pencil.)
- J'ai deux soeurs. (I have two sisters.)
- J'ai mal à l'estomac. (I have a stomach ache.)
- J'ai une question. (I have a question.)

▶ Conjugations of *Avoir*

Noun	Ending	Noun	Ending
je	ai	nous	avons
tu	as	vous	avez
il/elle	a	ils/elles	ont

Devoir—Should, Must, To Have To

The French verb *devoir* has a number of different meanings related to concepts like obligation, probability, expectation, and inevitability.

- Dois-tu étudier ce soir? (Do you have to study tonight?)
- Elles doivent partir. (They must/need to leave.)
- Nous devons travailler plus. (We should work more.)
- Elle doit être à l'école. (She must be at school.)

▶ Conjugations for *Devoir*

Noun	Ending	Noun	Ending
je	dois	nous	devons
tu	dois	vous	devez
il/elle	doit	ils/elles	doivent

Être—To Be

Être means "to be" in many senses that this verb is used in English. It is used with adjectives, nouns, and adverbs to describe a temporary or permanent state of being:

- Il est intelligent. (He is smart.)
- Je suis à Rome. (I'm in Rome.)
- Nous sommes américains. (We're American.)
- Il est ici. (He's here.)

Keep in mind that *être* is the auxiliary for some verbs in the compound tenses:

- Je suis allé en France. (I went to France.)
- Il était déjà sorti. (He had already left.)

Être is also used to form the passive voice:

- Les vêtement sont lavés. (The clothes are washed.)
- Elle est respectée de ses étudiants.
  (She is respected by her students.)

▶ Conjugations of *Être*

Noun	Ending	Noun	Ending
je	suis	nous	sommes
tu	es	vous	êtes
il/elle	est	ils/elles	sont

Faire—To Do, Make

Faire literally means "to do" or "to make" in most senses that these verbs are used in English.

- Je fais la vaisselle. (I'm doing the dishes.)
- Je fais de mon mieux. (I'm doing my best.)
- Je fais le lit. (I'm making the bed.)
- Je fais des projets. (I'm making plans.)

▶ **Conjugation of *Faire***

Noun	Ending	Noun	Ending
je	fais	nous	faisons
tu	fais	vous	faites
il/elle	fait	ils/elles	font

Pouvoir—Can, To Be Able to

The French verb *pouvoir* has a number of different meanings, depending mainly on the tense and mood it is conjugated into. In general, *pouvoir* means "to be able to," and is usually translated by "can," "could," or "may."

- Il peut nous aider. (He can help us.)
- Puis-je m'asseoir ici? (May I sit here?)
- Tu pourrais essayer. (You could try.)
- Pourriez-vous m'aider? (Could you help me?)

▶ **Conjugations of *Pouvoir*:**

Noun	Ending	Noun	Ending
je	peux	nous	pouvens
tu	peux	vous	pouvez
il/elle	peut	ils/elles	peuvent

Savoir and Connaître—To Know

The verbs *savoir* and *connaître* are both translated by the English verb "to know." This might seem confusing to you at first, but once you learn the difference in meaning and usage for the two verbs you shouldn't have any trouble.

Savoir means to know:

- a fact
- how to do something

Savoir is often followed by an infinitive or a subordinate clause.

- Je sais où il est. (I know where he is.)
- Sais-tu danser? (Do you know how to dance?)

▶ Conjugations of *Savoir*

Noun	Ending	Noun	Ending
je	sais	nous	savons
tu	sais	vous	savez
il/elle	sait	ils/elles	savent

Connaître means:

- to know (someone)
- to be familiar with (someone or something)

Connaître always has a direct object.

- Je connais tes frères. (I know your brothers.)
- Je connais cette histoire.
  (I am familiar with this story.)

▶ Conjugations of *Connaitre*:

Noun	Ending	Noun	Ending
je	connais	nous	connaissons
tu	connais	vous	connaissez
il/elle	connaît	ils/elles	connaissent

Venir—To Come

The irregular French verb *venir* means "to come" and is used just like its English equivalent.

▦ Il vient demain. (He's coming tomorrow.)
▦ Je viens d'Espagne. (I'm from/I come from Spain.)

▶ Conjugations of *Venir*

Noun	Ending	Noun	Ending
je	viens	nous	venons
tu	viens	vous	venez
il/elle	vient	ils/elles	viennent

Vouloir—To Want

The French verb *vouloir* means "to want":

▦ Je veux partir. (I want to leave.)
▦ Voulez-vous essayer? (Do you want to try?)

▶ Conjugations of *Vouloir*

Noun	Ending	Noun	Ending
je	veux	nous	voulons
tu	veux	vous	voulez
il/elle	veut	ils/elles	veulent

Simple Verb Tenses

A simple verb tense has a single conjugated verb, as opposed to a compound tense, which has two verbs (an auxiliary and a participle). The present tense is the most common simple tense. Some other simple tenses are the imperfect, future, conditional, and simple past.

Imperfect—l'imparfait

The imperfect tense is used to talk about a past action or state of being without specifying when it began or ended. It is often equivalent to "was ___-ing" in English.

The imperfect is relatively easy to conjugate because all verbs—regular, stem-changing, and irregular—except *être* are conjugated the same way: by dropping the *-ons* from the present-tense *nous* form and adding the appropriate ending.

▶ **Imperfect Conjugations**

Pronoun	Ending	Pronoun	Ending
je	-ais	nous	-ions
tu	-ais	vous	-iez
il/elle	-ait	ils/elles	-aient

Here is an example of imperfect conjugations for *-er*, *-ir*, and *-re* verbs as well as *être*.

▶ **Examples or *-er*, *-ir*, and *-re* Verbs**

	Parler	Finir	Rendre	Être
je (j')	parlais	finissais	rendais	étais
tu	parlais	finissais	rendais	étais
il/elle	parlait	finissait	rendait	était
nous	parlions	finissions	rendions	étions
vous	parliez	finissiez	rendiez	étiez
ils/elles	parlaient	finissaient	rendaient	étaient

Future—Le Futur

The future tense indicates something that is going to happen in the future and is usually equivalent to "will" in English:

- ▦ Ils étudieront plus tard. (They will study later.)
- ▦ J'irai à la banque demain.
  (I'll go to the bank tomorrow.)

▶ Future Endings

Pronoun	Ending	Pronoun	Ending
je	-ai	nous	-ons
tu	-as	vous	-ez
il/elle	-a	ils/elles	-ont

▶ Examples of *-er*, *-ir*, *-re*, stem-changing, and irregular verbs in the future tense

	Parler	*Choisir*	*Rendre*	*Lever*	*Aller*
je (j')	parlerai	choisirai	rendrai	lèverai	irai
tu	parleras	choisiras	rendras	lèveras	iras
il/elle	parlera	choisira	rendra	lèvera	ira
nous	parlerons	choisirons	rendrons	lèverons	irons
vous	parlerez	choisirez	rendrez	lèverez	irez
ils/elles	parleront	choisiront	rendront	lèveront	iront

Conditional—Le Conditionnel

The conditional is a verb mood used for actions that are not guaranteed to occur; often they depend on certain conditions. It is translated by "would" in English.

- ▦ J'achèterais la chemise bleue.
  (I would buy the blue shirt.)
- ▦ Nous devrions partir à midi.
  (We would have to leave at noon.)

The verb *vouloir* is used in the conditional to express a polite request:

- Je voudrais un verre de vin.
  (I would like a glass of wine.)
- Je voudrais le faire moi-même.
  (I would like to do it myself.)

The verb *aimer* is used in the conditional to express a polite desire, sometimes one that cannot be fulfilled:

- J'aimerais bien le voir!
  (I would really like to see it/him!)
- Il aimerait jouer, mais il doit travailler.
  (He would like to play, but he has to work.)

The conditional is conjugated with the infinitive or irregular conditional stem plus the conditional ending:

▶ Conditional Endings

Pronoun	Ending	Pronoun	Ending
je	-ais	nous	-ions
tu	-ais	vous	-iez
il/elle	-ait	ils/elles	-aient

Examples of *-er*, *-ir*, *-re*, stem-changing, and irregular verbs in the conditional

	Parler	Choisir	Rendre	Lever	Aller
je (j')	parlerais	choisirais	rendrais	lèverais	irais
tu	parlerais	choisirais	rendrais	lèverais	irais
il/elle	parlerait	choisirait	rendrait	lèverait	irait
nous	parlerions	choisirions	rendrions	lèverions	irions
vous	parleriez	choisiriez	rendriez	lèveriez	iriez
ils/elles	parleraient	choisiraient	rendraient	lèveraient	iraient

Present Participle—Le Participe Présent

The English present participle is the "-ing" form of a verb. The French present participle is formed by dropping *-ons* from the *nous* form of the present tense and adding *-ant*, for all but three verbs.

▶ Present Participle

	Parler	*Finir*	*Vendre*	*Devoir*
nous (present)	parlons	finissons	vendons	devons
present participle	parlant	finissant	vendant	devant

The three exceptions are:

- avoir   ayant
- être   étant
- savoir   sachant

For pronominal verbs, the present participle includes the reflexive pronoun.

- se lever   s'habiller
- se levant   s'habillant

Past Participle—Le Participe Passé

The English past participle is the *-ed* or *-en* form of the verb. In French, the past participle of regular verbs is formed by dropping the infinitive ending of a verb and adding the past participle ending: *é* for *-er* verbs, *i* for *-ir* verbs, and *u* for *-re* verbs.

▶ To Form the Past Participle

	Parler	Réussir	Vendre
1. remove	-er	-ir	-re
2. stem	parl-	réuss-	vend-
3. add	é	i	u
4. past participle	parlé	réussi	vendu

Most irregular verbs have irregular past participles so make sure to look them up!

The past participle has three main uses in French:

1. In conjunction with an auxiliary verb, the past participle forms compound tenses:

- J'ai étudié hier. (I studied yesterday.)
- Il est arrivé à minuit. (He arrived at midnight.)

2. With *être*, it forms the French passive voice.

- Le courrier est livré à deux heures.
- The mail is delivered at two o'clock.

3. By itself or accompanied by *être*, the French past participle may serve as an adjective. Note that in some cases, the *participe passé* may be translated by the English present participle.

- Déçu, j'ai pleuré pendant deux heures.
  (Disappointed, I cried for two hours.)
- La fille effrayée a crié.
  (The frightened girl screamed.)

When the past participle is used in the passive voice or as an adjective, it needs to agree in gender and number with the word it modifies. In the compound tenses, it may or may not need to agree, depending on certain factors.

Compound Verb Tenses

Compound verb tenses and moods are those made up of two parts: an auxiliary (helping) verb and a past participle. The auxiliary verb is what actually sets the tense and mood of the action—it must be conjugated according to the tense, mood, and voice of the action as well as to the subject.

Auxiliary Verbs—Les Auxiliaires

French has two auxiliary verbs used to conjugate the compound tenses, and all French verbs are classified by which auxiliary verb they take. Most French verbs use *avoir*, but the following verbs, generally verbs of motion, require être:

▶ **Verbs That Require *Être***

French	English
aller	to go
arriver	to arrive
descendre	to descend, to go down
entrer	to enter
monter	to climb, to go up
mourir	to die
naître	to be born
partir	to leave
passer	to spend (time)
rester	to stay
retourner	to return
sortir	to go out
tomber	to fall
venir	to come

These verbs, known as *être* verbs, are intransitive. However, when they are used transitively, the auxiliary is *avoir*.

- Je suis monté hier. (I went up yesterday.)
- J'ai monté la valise. (I took the suitcase up.)

In addition to the above verbs, all reflexive verbs take *être* in the compound tenses.

Compound Past Tense—Le Passé Composé

The French *passé composé* is equivalent in English to the simple past (I ate) and the present perfect (I have eaten). In French, both of these sentences would be translated *j'ai mangé*. The *passé composé* is the most common French past tense, often used in conjunction with the imperfect. It can express:

1. An action or state of being completed in the past:

- As-tu nagé ce weekend?
  (Did you swim this weekend?)
- Il est déjà parti. (He already left.)

2. An action repeated a specific number of times in the past:

- Hier, je suis tombé trois fois.
  (I fell three times yesterday.)
- Nous avons visité Paris plusieurs fois.
  (We've visited Paris several times.)

3. A series of actions completed in the past:

- Je suis allé à la banque et puis j'ai étudié.
  (I went to the bank and then I studied.)
- Il a vu sa mére, aparlé au médecin et a trouvé un chat.
  (He saw his mother, talked to a doctor, and found a
  cat.)

The passé composé is often used in conjunction with
the imperfect; both express past actions and states of being
but are used differently. The imperfect is used to express
ongoing actions with no specified completion, habitual
or repeated actions, background information, and general descriptions; the passé composé denotes events with
a definite beginning and end, single events, actions that
interrupted something, and changes in physical or mental
states. In general, the imperfect describes situations and
the passé composé narrates events.

The passé composé is conjugated with the present
tense of the appropriate auxiliary verb plus the past participle.

▶ **Parler**

Noun	Ending	Noun	Ending
j'	ai parlé	nous	avons parlé
tu	as parlé	vous	avez parlé
il/elle	a parlé	ils/elles	ont parlé

▶ **Sortir**

Noun	Ending	Noun	Ending
je	suis sorti(e)	nous	sommes sorti(e)s
tu	es sorti(e)	vous	êtes sorti(e)(s
il/elle	est sorti(e)	ils/elles	sont sorti(e)(s)

▶ *Se Laver*

Noun	Ending	Noun	Ending
je	me suis lavé(e)	nous	nous sommes lavé(e)s
tu	t'es lavé(e)	vous	vous êtes lavé(e)(s)
il/elle	s'est lavé(e)	ils/elles	se sont lavé(e)s

The letters in parentheses indicate grammatical agreement—the conjugation depends on the word the verb is modifying.

Pluperfect (Past Perfect)—Le Plus-Que-Parfait

The French pluperfect is used to talk about an action in the past that occurred before another action in the past. The latter can be either mentioned in the same sentence or implied.

- Il n'avait pas mangé (avant de sortir).
  (He hadn't eaten [before going out].)
- J'étais déjà sorti (quand tu as téléphoné).
  (I had already left [when you called].)

The pluperfect is conjugated with the imperfect of the appropriate auxiliary verb plus the past participle of the action verb.

▶ *Parler*

Noun	Ending	Noun	Ending
j'	avais parlé	nous	avions parlé
tu	avais parlé	vous	aviez parlé
il/elle	avait parlé	ils/elles	avaient parlé

▶ *Sortir*

Noun	Ending	Noun	Ending
j'	étais sorti(e)	nous	étions sorti(e)s
tu	étais sorti(e)	vous	étiez sorti(e)(s)
il/elle	était sorti(e)	ils/elles	étaient sorti(e)s

▶ *Se Laver*

Noun	Ending	Noun	Ending
je	m'étais lavé(e)	nous	nous étions lavé(e)s
tu	t'étais lavé(e)	vous	vous étiez lavé(e)s
il/elle	s'était lavé(e)	ils/elles	s'étaient lavé(e)s

Future perfect—Le Futur Antérieur

The future perfect is mainly used to describe an action that will have happened by a specific point in the future.

- ▪ J'aurai fini à trois heures.
  (I will have finished at three o'clock.)
- ▪ Dans une semaine, il sera né.
  (In a week, he will have been born.)

The French future perfect is conjugated with the auxiliary verb in the future plus the past participle.

▶ *Aimer*

Noun	Ending	Noun	Ending
j'	aurai aimé	nous	aurons aimé
tu	auras aimé	vous	aurez aimé
il/elle	aura aimé	ils/elles	auront aimé

▶ *Venir*

Noun	Ending	Noun	Ending
je	serai venu(e)	nous	serons venu(e)s
tu	seras venu(e)	vous	serez venu(e)(s)
il/elle	sera venu(e)	ils/elles	seront venu(e)s

▶ Se Laver

Noun	Ending	Noun	Ending
je	me serai lavé(e)	nous	nous serons lavé(e)s
tu	te seras lavé(e)	vous	vous serez lavé(e)(s)
il/elle	se sera lavé(e)	ils/elles	se seront lavé(e)s

Conditional Perfect (Past Conditional)—Le Conditionnel Parfait

The French conditional perfect is used just like the English conditional perfect—to express actions that would have occurred in the past if circumstances had been different.

The conditional perfect is often used for the result clause in *si* clauses with the unmet condition in the pluperfect:

- Si j'avais mangé, je ne me serais pas évanoui.
  (If I had eaten, I wouldn't have fainted.)
- Il serait tombé si tu l'avais poussé.
  (He would have fallen if you had pushed him.)

The conditional perfect can be used to indicate a better alternative than what actually happened in the past, or it can express an unrealized desire in the past, or it can report an uncertain or unverified statement, especially in the news.

The conditional perfect is formed with the auxiliary verb in the condition tense plus the past participle.

▶ Aimer

Noun	Ending	Noun	Ending
j'	aurais aimé	nous	aurions aimé
tu	aurais aimé	vous	auriez aimé
il/elle	aurait aimé	ils/elles	auraientt aimé

▶ *Venir*

Noun	Ending	Noun	Ending
je	serais venu(e)	nous	serions venu(e)s
tu	serais venu(e)	vous	seriez venu(e)(s)
il/elle	serait venu(e)	ils/elles	seraient venu(e)s

▶ *Se Laver*

Noun	Ending	Noun	Ending
je	me serais lavé(e)	nous	nous serions lavé(e)s
tu	te serais lavé(e)	vous	vous seriez lavé(e)(s)
il/elle	se serait lavé(e)	ils/elles	se seraient lavé(e)s

Imperative—L'impératif

The imperative is the verb mood used to give a command, either affirmative (Go!) or negative (Don't go!). There are only three forms of the imperative (*tu, nous,* and *vous*) and their conjugations are among the easiest in French. Take a look.

▶ **Examples of the French imperative**

	Parler	*Finir*	*Attendre*
(tu)	parle	finis	attends
(nous)	parlons	finissons	attendons
(vous)	parlez	finissez	attendez

There are only four verbs with irregular forms in the imperative.

	Avoir	*Être*	*Savoir*	*Vouloir*
(tu)	aie	sois	sache	veuille
(nous)	ayons	soyons	sachons	n/a
(vous)	ayez	soyez	sachez	veuillez

Reflexive verbs in the imperative are followed by their reflexive pronoun and joined by a hyphen.

infinitive	se lever	s'habiller
(tu)	lève-toi	habille-toi
(nous)	levons-nous	habillons-nous
(vous)	levez-vous	habillez-vous

Subjunctive—Le Subjonctif

The subjunctive mood is subjective: it expresses emotional, potential, and hypothetical attitudes about what is being expressed—things like will/wanting, emotion, doubt, possibility, necessity, and judgment. The subjunctive is required after many verbs, conjunctions, and impersonal expressions.

- Je veux que tu viennes. (I want you to come.)
- J'ai peur qu'il soit malade. (I'm afraid he is sick.)

The subjunctive endings are the same for regular, stem-changing, and irregular verbs, but the stem varies. Take a look.

▶ Subjunctive

	Ending	Parler	Choisir	Rendre
…que je	-e	parle	choisisse	rende
…que tu	-es	parles	choisisses	rendes
…qu'il/elle	-e	parle	choisisse	rende
…que nous	-ions	parlions	choisissions	rendions
…que vous	-iez	parliez	choisissiez	rendiez
…qu'ils/elles	−ent	parlent	choisissent	rendent

Subjunctive conjugations of verbs are used for both the present and future—there is no future subjunctive. Stem-changing verbs and many irregular verbs follow the same pattern as regular verbs for the singular conjugations (*je, tu, il/elle*) and the third person plural (*ils/elles*).

But for the *nous* and *vous* forms of the subjunctive, they use the first person plural (*nous*) as the stem:

▶ Subjunctive Irregulars

	Envoyer	Jeter	Prendre	Venir
…que je (j')	envoie	jette	prenne	vienne
…que tu	envoies	jettes	prennes	viennes
…qu'il/elle	envoie	jette	prenne	vienne
…que nous	envoyions	jetions	prenions	venions
…que vous	envoyiez	jetiez	preniez	veniez
…qu'ils/elles	envoient	jettent	prennent	viennent

Other irregular verbs that follow this pattern are *boire, croire, devoir, mourir, recevoir,* and *voir. Aller* and *vouloir* each have two irregular stems but follow the above pattern and take the same endings.

▶ *Aller* and *Vouloir* Endings

	Aller	Vouloir
…que je (j')	aille	veuille
…que tu	ailles	veuilles
…qu'il/elle	aille	veuille
…que nous	allions	voulions
…que vous	alliez	vouliez
…qu'ils/elles	aillent	veuillent

Three verbs have a single irregular stem but use the same endings:

	Faire	Pouvoir	Savoir
…que je (j')	fasse	puisse	sache
…que tu	fasses	puisses	saches
…qu'il/elle	fasse	puisse	sache
…que nous	fassions	puissions	sachions
…que vous	fassiez	puissiez	sachiez
…qu'ils/elles	fassent	puissent	sachent

Avoir and *être* are completely irregular in the subjunctive.

	Avoir	Etre
...que je (j')	aie	sois
...que tu	aies	sois
...qu'il/elle	ait	soit
...que nous	ayons	soyons
...que vous	ayez	soyez
...qu'ils/elles	aient	soient

Voice—La Voix

Voice indicates the relationship between the subject and verb—who is performing the action on whom. There are three French voices:

1. **Active**—The subject performs the action of the verb. Active is the most typical, "normal" voice.

- Je répare la voiture. (I'm repairing the car.)
- Il habille le bébé. (He's dressing the baby.)

2. **Passive**—The action of the verb is performed on the subject by an agent.

- La voiture est réparée. (The car is (being) repaired.)
- La souris est mangée par le chat.
  (The mouse is eaten by the cat.)

3. **Reflexive**—The subject performs the action on itself.

- Je me lave. (I'm washing up.)
- Il s'habille. (He's getting dressed.)

Everything you've seen so far in this book has been in the active voice, with the exception of pronominal verbs (reflexive voice). Now you need to understand passive voice.

The passive voice is formed with *être* conjugated into the appropriate tense, followed by the past participle. It exists in all tenses and moods, as you can see here with *faire le lit* (to make the bed). However, it is not very commonly used.

▶ Active and Passive

	Active	Passive
Present	je fais le lit	le lit est fait par moi
Passé Composé	j'ai fait le lit	le lit a été fait par moi
Imperfect	je faisais le lit	le lit était fait par moi
Future	je ferai le lit	le lit sera fait par moi
Subjunctive	que je fasse le lit	que le lit soit fait par moi

The passive voice always has one more verb (the auxiliary verb *être*) than the active voice. In the passive voice, the action described by the verb is being done to the subject by an agent, which may or may not be stated.

Questions

Asking questions can be difficult in any language, because there are usually several different types of interrogative constructions, special interrogatory words may be required, and the word order is usually different for questions and statements.

There are four ways to ask questions in French. The four different constructions are listed in order, from formal to informal.

1. Invert the subject and verb and join them with a hyphen.

■ Comprends-tu? (Do you understand?)
■ As-tu compris? (Did you understand?)

2. Put *est-ce que* at the beginning of any sentence:

■ Est-ce que tu comprends? (Do you understand?)
■ Est-ce que tu as compris? (Did you understand?)

3. Add the tag *n'est-ce pas* to the end of the sentence (when you expect the answer to be *yes*):

■ Tu comprends, n'est-ce pas? (You understand, right?)
■ Tu as compris, n'est-ce pas? (You understood, right?)

4. Raise the pitch of your voice at the end of any sentence:

■ Tu comprends? (You understand?)
■ Tu as compris? (You understood?)

Yes/No Questions

Questions to which the answer is *yes* or *no* are the simplest. You can use any of the above constructions and you can answer with a simple *oui* or *non*, or by restating the question as a statement.

Question
Aimes-tu danser? Do you like to dance? *Est-ce que tu aimes danser?*

Possible answers
■ Oui. (Yes.)
■ Oui, j'aime danser. (Yes, I like to dance.)

- Non. (No.)
- Non, je n'aime pas danser. (No, I don't like to dance.)

Interrogative Adverbs

Interrogative adverbs are used to ask for new information or facts, whereas regular interrogative questions lead to a "yes" or "no" answer. These useful words will help you elicit more detailed information about a subject.

▶ Adverbs Used to Ask Questions

French	English
combien de	how many/much
comment	how
où	where
pourquoi	why
quand	when

All of these can be used with either *est-ce que* or inversion. Here are examples of how you can ask the same question using both *est-ce que* and inversion:

- Où habites-tu?/Où est-ce que tu habites?
  (Where do you live?)
- Quand manges-tu?/Quand est-ce que tu manges?
  (When do you eat?)

Interrogative Adjectives

When it comes to interrogative adjectives, French grammar is much more strict than English grammar. In English, you can say "What book do you want?" and no one will raise an eyebrow, though technically it is grammatically incorrect. In proper English, the question should be "Which book do you want?" but in reality, "what book" is much more common. In French, however, you do not have this option: the French equivalent of which, *quel*, must be used whenever there is more than one noun that you are choosing from—thus, "*Quel livre?*" *Quel* + noun is replaced by the interrogative pronoun *lequel*. *Quel livre veux-tu? Lequel veux-tu?*

- Quelle heure est-il? (What time is it?)
- Dans quel magasin travaille-t-il?
  (What store does he work in?)
- Ana m'a prêté une voiture. (Ana loaned me a car.)
- Quelle voiture? (What (which) car?)

Quel can be used with inversion or *est-ce que*:

- Quel verre veux-tu? (What glass do you want?)
- Quel verre est-ce que tu veux?
  (What glass do you want?)

Quel can be used after a preposition:

- À quelle heure va-t-il arriver?
  (What time is he going to arrive?)
- De quels étudiants est-ce qu'il parle?
  (What students is he talking about?)

Quel followed by *être*:

- Quel est le problème? (What's the problem?)
- Quelle est votre question? (What's your question?)

More Questions: Interrogative Pronouns
Interrogative pronouns ask "who," "what," or "which one." The three French interrogative pronouns are *qui, que*, and *lequel* and all three of them can also be relative pronouns.

Qui

Qui means "who" or "whom" and is used to ask about people.

- Qui êtes-vous? (Who are you?)
- Qui est là? (Who's there?)

When "whom" is the object of the question, *qui* can be followed by either *est-ce que* or inversion.

- Qui est-ce que vous aimez? Qui aimez-vous? (Whom do you love?)
- Qui est-ce qu'il a vu? Qui a-t-il vu? (Whom did he see?)

When "who" is the subject of the question, you can use either *qui* or *qui est-ce qui*. The word order cannot be inverted and the verb is always in the third person singular.

- Qui (est-ce qui) veut étudier le français? (Who wants to study French?)
- Qui (est-ce qui) vient avec nous? (Who is coming with us?)

When *qui* follows a preposition, you can use inversion or *est-ce que*.

- À qui est-ce que tu parles? À qui parles-tu?
- To whom are you speaking?

Que

Que means "what" and is used to refer to ideas or objects. When "what" is the object of the question, it can be followed by inversion or *est-ce que*.

■ Qu'est-ce qu'elle cherche? Que cherche-t-elle?
(What is she looking for?)
■ Qu'est-ce que c'est (que cela)? (What is that?)

When "what" is the subject of the question, *qu'est-ce qui* must be used, followed by a third person singular verb, with no inversion.

■ Qu'est-ce qui se passe? (What's happening?)
■ Qu'est-ce qui a pu faire cela?
(What could have done this?)

After a preposition, *que* changes to *quoi*.

■ Avec quoi est-ce que vous écrivez? Avec quoi écrivez-vous?
■ What are you writing with?

■ À quoi est-ce que tu penses? À quoi penses-tu?
■ What are you thinking about?

Negation

No matter how positive positive and optimistic you are, sometimes you just have to say no. In this chapter, you'll learn all about how to be grammatically negative in French. There are a variety of ways to make a statement negative in French, and each construction is used for specific situations.

With a little practice, you will be able to respond easily with the proper form of negation.

Ne...pas and Other Negative Adverbs

Negative adverbs are the constructions used to negate the action or state of a verb. The English negative adverb is "not," as in "I'm not going, I don't (do not) have time." In French, it's a little bit more complicated.

The French equivalent of "not" is the two-part construction *ne...pas*, which surrounds the verb being negated. To make a sentence or question negative, place *ne* in front of the conjugated verb and *pas* after it.

- Je suis grand—Je ne suis pas grand.
  (I'm tall—I'm not tall.)
- Vous êtes fatigué?—Vous n'êtes pas fatigué?
  (Are you tired?—Aren't you tired?)

In dual-verb and compound tense constructions, *ne... pas* surrounds the conjugated verb.

- Il veut jouer—Il ne veut pas jouer.
- He wants to play—He doesn't want to play.
- J'ai mangé—Je n'ai pas mangé.
- I ate—I didn't eat.

When negating an infinitive, *ne pas* stays together in front of the verb: *J'ai décidé de ne pas accepter.* (I decided not to accept.) *Ne...pas* is the most common negative adverb, but there are a number of others, all of which follow the above placement rules.

- ne...pas encore (not yet)
- Il n'a pas encore mangé. (He hasn't eaten yet.)

Pas without Ne

There are two types of situations in which *pas* is used without *ne*, including informal negation and nonverbal negation.

Informal Negation

On the opposite end of the spectrum from the formal negative structures in the previous section, you have informal French, in which *ne* is often dropped, leaving only *pas* to make the statement negative. Although *ne* is nearly always written, it is often dropped in spoken French.

- Je ne suis pas prêt—Je suis pas prêt. (I'm not ready.)
- Tu ne peux pas y aller? Tu peux pas y aller?
  (You can't go?)
- Ne mange pas ça!—Mange pas ça! (Don't eat that!)
- Je n'ai jamais fait ça.—J'ai jamais fait ça.
  (I've never done that.)

Nonverbal Negation

When negating an adjective, adverb, noun, or some other nonverbal construction, *pas* is used on its own, paired with an adjective, adverb, noun, or pronoun.

Pas + adjective
- Pas parfait, mais ça marche. (Not perfect, but it works.)
- Pas bon, ça. (That's not good.)
- C'est un garçon pas gentil. (He is an unkind boy.)

Pas + adverb
- Pas trop. (Not too much.)
- Pas mal. (Not bad.)
- Pourquoi pas? (Why not?)

Pas + noun

- ▦ Tu viens demain? (Are you coming tomorrow?)
- ▦ Non, pas demain. lundi. (No, not tomorrow. Monday.)
- ▦ Pas de problème! (No problem!)

Pas + pronoun

- ▦ J'ai faim, pas toi? (I'm hungry, aren't you?)
- ▦ Pas moi! (Not me!)
- ▦ Pas ceci; je veux cela. (Not this; I want that.)

Pas can also be used to confirm a statement.

- ▦ Tu comprends, ou pas? (Do you understand, or not?)
- ▦ Je veux le faire, pas toi? (I want to do it, don't you?)
- ▦ Pas juste? (Right? Isn't that cor-rect?)

Negative Adjectives

Like negative adverbs, French negative adjectives are composed of two words that surround the verb. Negative adjectives negate, refuse, or cast doubt on a quality of the noun they modify.

- ▦ Vous n'avez aucune preuve. (You don't have any proof.)
- ▦ Je ne connais pas un seul avocat. (I don't know a single lawyer.)
- ▦ Pas un problème n'a été résolu. (No problem has been resolved.)

There are four French negative adjectives:

- ▦ ne...aucun(e) (no, not any)
- ▦ ne...nul(le) (no, not any)
- ▦ ne...pas un(e) (no, not one)
- ▦ ne...pas un(e) seul(e) (not a single)

All of these mean more or less the same thing, with *ne...pas un seul* being just a bit stronger. However, *pas un* and *pas un seul* are used only for countable nouns (people, cars), *nul* is used only for collective nouns (money, time), and *aucun* can be used for both countable and collective nouns.

The parentheses indicate the letters that need to be added when negating a feminine noun because, like all adjectives, negative adjectives must agree in gender and number with the nouns that they modify. When a negative adjective modifies the subject of the sentence, the verb must be conjugated in the third person singular.

■ Pas une seule femme ne le sait.
  (Not a single woman knows it.)
■ Aucune femme ne le veut. (No woman wants it.)
■ Aucun argent n'a été retrouvé.
  (No money was found.)

Negative Pronouns

Like adjectives and adverbs, French negative pronouns consist of two parts that surround the verb. Negative pronouns are used to negate, refuse, or cast doubt on the existence of the noun that they replace.

■ Elles n'ont vu aucun des films.
  (They haven't seen any of the movies.)
■ Je n'ai rien fait.
  (I haven't done anything. / I have done nothing.)
■ Nous ne connaissons personne.
  (We don't know anyone.)

▶ French Negative Pronouns

French	English
ne...aucun(e) (de)	none (of), not any (of)
ne...nul(le)	no one
ne...pas un(e) (de)	not one (of)
ne...pas un(e) seul(e) (de)	not a single one (of)
ne...personne	no one
ne...rien	nothing, not...anything

Negative pronouns can be the subject, direct object, or indirect object of a sentence.

- Rien n'a été fait. (Nothing was done.)
- Je n'ai rien fait. (I didn't do anything.)
- Je ne pense à personne. (I'm not thinking about anyone.)

The negative conjunction *ne...ni...ni* means "neither...nor" and is used just like negative pronouns, with *ne* preceding the verb and each *ni* preceding one of the negated words.

- Il n'est ni intelligent ni créatif.
  (He is neither intelligent nor creative.)
- Ni Jacques ni Luc ne sont venus.
  (Neither Jacques nor Luc came.)

Presentatives and Determiners

Presentatives and determiners are two related categories of terms that introduce nouns while emphasizing or modifying them. Presentatives simultaneously introduce and emphasize something. Determiners, on the other hand, introduce and at the same time modify nouns. Both groups of words are helpful to know and help you avoid confusion when you are trying to understand fluent French speakers.

Introduction to Presentatives

While they are significant words that serve multiple functions, presentatives are not a part of speech so much as a small group of assorted terms used in this way, including prepositions, conjunctions, adverbs, and expressions.

▶ **Presentatives**

French	English
à	to
À table!	(come) to the table!
à bas	down with
À bas le fascisme!	Down with fascism!
c'est, ce sont	this/it is, these are
C'est une bonne histoire.	It's a good story.
il y a	there is/are
Il y a trois chaises.	There are three chairs.
voici	here is/are
Voici ma voiture.	Here is my car.
voilà	there is
Voilà la maison.	There's the house (over there)

C'est and Il est

C'est and *il est* are two of the most important French presentatives. They may be translated by "this/that/it is," "they are," or "he/she is."

▪ Votre village? C'est très joli!
(Your village? It's very pretty!)

■ Il est difficile d'être honnête.
   (It's difficult to be honest.)
■ Ana? C'est une fille sympa. (Ana? She's a nice girl.)
■ Il est tard. (It's late.)

Don't forget, *c'est* normally becomes *ce sont* when followed by a plural noun.

Although the expressions *c'est* and *il est* have similar meanings, they cannot be used interchangeably. In fact, the rules for their usage are quite strict. Let's start by looking at *c'est*, which can be followed by the following terms.

A Modified Noun
■ C'est un avocat. (He's a lawyer.)
■ C'est mon frère. (That's my brother.)

An Adjective
■ C'est bon. (It's good.)
■ Ce n'est pas évident. (It's not easy.)

A Modified Adverb
■ C'est trop tard. (It's very late.)
■ C'est trop loin. (It is too far away.)

A Proper Name
■ C'est Michel. (It's Michel.)
■ Ce sont Laure et Marie. (It is Laure and Marie.)

A Stressed Pronoun
■ C'est moi. (It's / That's me.)
■ C'est lui qui veut y aller. (It's him that wants to go.)

Now let's take a look at *Il est*. It can be used with the following terms.

An Unmodified Noun
- Il est avocat. (He's a lawyer.)
- Elle est actrice. (She's an actress.)

An Adjective (person)
- Il est sportif. (He is athletic.)
- Elle est belle. (She is beautiful.)

An Unmodified Adverb
- Il est tard. (It's late.)
- Elles sont ici. (They are here.)

A Prepositional Phrase
- Il est en France. (He's in France.)
- Elle est à l'école (She is at school.)

Il y a

Il y a is another extremely important French expression. *Il y a* means "there is" or "there are" and is usually followed by an indefinite article, adjective, or pronoun, or a number + noun.

- Il y a un livre sur la table.
  (There's a book on the table.)
- Il y a plusieurs choses à faire.
  (There are several things to do.)

It might help you to understand the three words that comprise the expression *il y a*:

1. *il*—the subject "it"
2. *y*—the pronoun "there"
3. *a*—the third person singular present tense of *avoir* (to have)

To make *il y a* negative, just place *n'* in front of *y* (because *ne* contracts to *n'* in front of *y* or a vowel) and place *pas* after *a*.

- Il n'y a pas de livre sur la table.
  (There isn't any book on the table.)
- Il n'y a pas de vêtements ici.
  (There aren't any clothes here.)

Remember that the indefinite article changes to *de* due to the negation.

To use *il y a* in another tense, you just conjugate *avoir* into that tense:

- Il y avait un livre… (There was a book…)
- Il y aura un livre… (There will be a book…)

You can ask a question with either use, *est-ce que* or inversion.

- Est-ce qu'il y a un livre? (Is there a book?)
- Est-ce qu'il y a des vêtements? (Are there any clothes?)

To invert *il y a*, start with the pronoun *y*, then invert *il* and *a*. This will give you two adjacent vowels (*a il*), so you will need to add *a t* surrounded with dashes between them:

- Y a-t-il un livre? (Is there a book?)
- Y a-t-il des vêtements? (Are there any clothes?)

You can also use *il y a* with interrogative words:

- Pourquoi est-ce qu'il y a un livre sur la table? (Why is there a book on the table?)
- Combien de livres y a-t-il? (How many books are there?)

When *il y a* is followed by a period of time, it means "ago."

- Je l'ai lu il y a deux semaines.
  (I read it two weeks ago.)
- Il y a un an que nous avons déménagé.
  (We moved a year ago.)

Voici and Voilà

Voici and *voilà* mean "here is" and "there is," respectively. *Voici* and *voilà* are used when the speaker is actually handing something to another person or pointing out to something or someone nearby.

- Voici vos clés. (Here are your keys.)
- Voilà ton père. (There's your father (over there).)

Voici and *voilà* are commonly preceded by the definite object or adverbial pronoun *en*.

- Où est mon sac? Le voilà. (Where is my bag? (It's) over there.)
- Tes livres? Les voici. (Your books? Here they are.)

In informal French, *voilà* is used considerably more often than *voici*—*voilà* tends to be used to mean both "here is" and "there is."

▓ Voilà ton ami qui arrive. (Your friend is here.)
▓ Où est-il? Le voilà. (Where is it? Here you go.)

Voilà can also be used to respond to some kind of demand or question.

▓ Voilà, j'arrive, j'arrive.
(All right, I'm coming, I'm coming.)
▓ Voilà, j'ai terminé! (There, I'm done!)
▓ Et voilà! (That's it!)

Introduction to Determiners

Determiners introduce and at the same time modify nouns. Determiners include articles and certain types of adjectives; in fact, determiners are sometimes referred to as non-qualifying adjectives. Determiners are much more common in French than in English—nearly every noun in a French sentence must be preceded by some sort of determiner. Unlike qualifying (descriptive) adjectives, determiners always precede the noun they modify, cannot be modified, and cannot be used with other determiners. All articles are determiners.

▶ Determiners

Article	Purpose	French	English
definite	refer to specific object	le, la, les	the
indefinite	refer to unspecified object	un, une, des	a, an, some
partitive	refer to unknown quantity	du, de la, des	some

Many types of adjectives are also determiners.

▶ Adjectives as Determiners

Adjective	Purpose	French	English
demonstrative	indicate specific noun	ce, cet, cette, ces	this, that, these, those

▶ Adjectives as Determiners (continued)

Adjective	Purpose	French	English
exclamative	express strong sentiment	quel(s), quelle(s)	what a
indefinite	modify without specifying	autre, certain	other, certain
interrogative	ask "which?"	quel(s), quelle(s)	which
negative	negate or cast doubt	ne...aucun, nul	no, not a single
possessive	indicate possessor	mon, ton, son	my, your, his

Possession

Expressing possession in French is similar in many ways to English. Both languages have possessive adjectives and pronouns, and both have a third way to express possession using a name or noun. The biggest difference is that English has a total of three ways to express possession, but French has four. It is the fourth method of French possession that is the trickiest for students.

Possessive Adjectives

Possessive adjectives are the determiners used to indicate to whom or to what something belongs. French and English possessive adjectives are used similarly, but French is a little more complicated when it comes to form: like most French adjectives, possessives have different forms for masculine and feminine, singular and plural.

▶ Possessive Adjectives

English	Masculine	Feminine	Before Vowel	Plural
my	mon	ma	mon	mes
your (tu form)	ton	ta	ton	tes
his, her, its	son	sa	son	ses

our	notre	notre	notre	nos
your (vous)	votre	votre	votre	vos
their	leur	leur	leur	leurs

▶ **Examples**

	Masculine	Feminine	Vowel	Plural
my	mon stylo	ma montre	mon amie	mes frères
your	ton stylo	ta montre	ton amie	tes frères
his, her, its	son stylo	sa montre	son amie	ses frères
our	notre livre	notre table	notre amie	nos tables
your	votre livre	votre table	votre amie	vos tables
their	leur livre	leur table	leur amie	leurs tables

Possessive adjectives are never used with any type of article; in fact, they replace the article: *un livre*—a book, *mon livre*—my book.

Possessive *De*
The French preposition *de* is used to express possession with a noun or name. This is equivalent to *'s* or *s'* in English.

- le livre de David (David's book)
- les musées de France (France's museums)
- les jouets de la fille (the girl's toys)
- les jouets des filles (the girls' toys)

Note that the order of the nouns is inverted in French. *Les musées de France* translates literally to "the museums of France."

The possessor noun must be preceded by an article: *les pages du livre* (the book's pages), *les pages d'un livre* (a book's pages) As with the partitive article and other de constructions, *de* contracts with *le* and *les* to make *du* and *des*.

Possessive Pronouns

Possessive pronouns replace possessive adjectives plus nouns. Once again, French has different forms of the possessive pronoun depending on the gender and number of the noun it is replacing.

▶ Possessive Pronouns

Singular		Plural		
Masculine	Feminine	Masculine	Feminine	
mine	le mien	la mienne	les miens	les miennes
yours (sing., fam.)	le tien	la tienne	les tiens	les tiennes
his/hers/its	le sien	la sienne	les siens	les siennes
ours	le nôtre	la nôtre	les nôtres	les nôtres
yours (plur., form.)	le vôtre	la vôtre	les vôtres	les vôtres
theirs	le leur	la leur	les leurs	les leurs

French and English possessive pronouns are very similar, with two exceptions: the French possessive pronoun must match the noun being replaced in number and gender, and a definite article must be used.

- Mes enfants sont en Italie. Où habitent les tiens?
- My kids are in Italy. Where do yours live?

- Cet argent…c'est le tien ou le mien?
- This money…is it yours or mine?

When the possessive pronoun is preceded by *à* or *de*, the preposition contracts with the definite article:

- Tu penses à ta décision; je dois penser à la mienne.

▓ You think about your decision; I need to think about mine.

▓ Ils parlent de leurs projets et nous parlons des nôtres.

▓ They are talking about their plans and we are talking about ours.

Possessive à

The possessive *à* can be used only after the verb *être* or after *c'est* + noun. It emphasizes the ownership of the object, such as when you are trying to determine to whom something belongs: *c'est à moi ou à toi?*—is it mine or yours? There are two constructions in which the possessive *à* replaces a different structure used in English.

1. Possessive *à* replaces possessive *de*.

The only time *'s* or *s'* can be translated by something other than the possessive *de* is in the English construction noun + of + name, in which case the possessive à is used: *un ami à Marie*—a friend of Marie (compare to *l'ami de Marie*—Marie's friend).

2. Possessive *à* replaces possessive pronoun.

To translate the English constructions noun + of + possessive pronoun and it is + possessive pronoun, French uses the possessive à: *un livre à moi*—a book of mine; *C'est à moi!*—It's mine!

04 / Putting It All Together

Writing in French
Writing in French can be a very different matter than speaking French. In addition, knowing how to write a word in French can very often help you better understand and remember its spoken form. By practicing writing in French, you may notice a similarity to the word's English counterpart, and the simple act of writing vocabulary helps you cement that word's meaning into memory.

Contractions
Contractions—the dropping of one or more letters and replacing them with an apostrophe—are optional in English but required in French. For example, in English you can say "I am" or "I'm"; the latter is somewhat less formal. In contrast, you cannot say "je ai" (I have) in French; you must make the contraction *j'ai*. There are three main types of French contractions:

1. Short, single-syllable words contract with the word that follows if it begins with a vowel or *h muet*.

▶ **Contractions**

Combination	Result	English
ce + est	c'est	it is
de + amour	d'amour	of/about love
je + habite	j'habite	I live
je le + ai	je l'ai	I have it
la + amie	l'amie	the friend
le + homme	l'homme	the man
que + il	qu'il	that it/ that he
il se + appelle	il s'appelle	his name is
je te + aime	je t'aime	I love you

2. The prepositions *à* and *de* contract with the definite articles *le* and *les*, but not with *la* or *l'*:

▶ **Article *à***

Combination	Result
à + le	au
à + les	aux
à + la	à la
à + l'	à l'

▶ ***De***

Combination	Result
de + le	du
de + les	des
de + la	de la
de + l'	de l'

3. Si contracts with *il* and *ils*, but not *elle(s)*:

▶ **Si**

Combination	Results	English
si + il	s'il	if he/it
si + ils	s'ils	if they
si + elle	si elle	if she/it
si + elles	si elles	if they

Capitalization

For the most part, French follows the same rules regarding capitalization as English, with a few exceptions. In French, a capital letter is known as a majuscule. Capitalized words are said to be *en majuscules*. The following shows the types of words that are capitalized in French:

- The first word in a sentence is capitalized.
- Both first and last names are capitalized.
- Names of cities, countries, and continents are capitalized.
- Directions are capitalized to indicate a specific place, like l'Amérique du Nord (North America). When used to indicate a general direction, like *le nord* (north), no majuscule is used.
- When words are used as nouns to indicate the nationality of a person, for example, un Français (a Frenchman), the word is capitalized.

Punctuation Marks

Written French looks very similar to English, so reading books in French should seem almost familiar. For the most part, French and Eglish use the same punctuation marks, and they function in much the same way as in English. Included in this section are the French terms for many punctuation marks; they are handy words to know, and you never can tell when you may be called upon to use them.

One-Part Punctuation

One-part punctuation marks are very similar in the two languages, so the summary for punctuation usage only covers the differences between French punctuation usage and that of English.

Period

The period (*le point*, in French) is used in some French countries and parts of Canada to separate numbers (10.000), rather than the comma that is used in English: 10,500. In France, however, a space is used in place of the English comma to separate thousands, for example, so a number such as 123,456 would become in French *123 456*. The period can also be used in French to separate dates: 6.12.05—*6 décembre 2005*. The period is not used after abbreviations of measurement or abbreviated titles, or as a decimal point: *20 min*–20 min., *Mme*—Mrs. (However for "*Monsieur*" the correct abbreviation is "M.")

Comma

The comma (*la virgule*, in French) is equivalent to the decimal point used in English: *7,25%*—7.25%.

Two-Part Punctuation Marks

In French, all punctuation marks and symbols with two or more parts, such as : ; « » !? % $ and #, must be preceded by a space: *Ça va? Très bien!*

Colon

The colon, called *les deux points* in French, is much more common in French than in English. It is used to introduce direct speech, where in English you would use a comma: *Il a dit : «Je veux le faire»*.—He said, "I want to do it."

The colon can also introduce the explanation, conclusion, or summary of whatever precedes it: *Ce livre est très bon : c'est un classique du genre.* (This book is very good; it's a classic of its kind.)

Quotation marks

Quotation marks (*les guillemets*) tend to be used only at the beginning and end of an entire conversation. This is quite different than the use of quotation marks in English, which surrounds each spoken word, phrase, or paragraph with quotation marks, which means that the quotation marks end each time there is an incidental clause like "he said" or "she replied," as well as any time the speaker changes. This is not the case in French. Instead, *les guillemets* surround the entire conversation and each new speaker is indicated by an m-dash (*un tiret*).

«Salut Marc! dit Anne. Ça va?
—Ah, salut Anne! répond Marc. Ça va bien, et toi?
—Oui, ça va.»

Punctuation Similarities

The following symbols are used more or less the same way in French and English, besides the fact that French inserts a space between the word and punctuation mark:

- le point-virgule (semi-colon)
- le point d'exclamation (exclamation point)
- le point d'interrogation (question mark)

Accents

In order to provide guides to pronunciation, French uses accents, which are pronunciation marks that appear with some letters. There are four accents commonly used with vowels: the grave accent, the acute accent, the circumflex, and the umlaut.

The Acute Accent

The acute accent, called *aigu* (ay-gooh) in French, points upward and toward the right, as in *é*. Although it only appears over the letter *e*, it can become an integral part of a word, substantially changing its meaning. The acute accent also provides important clues about where the word fits in a sentence. Whenever it appears, it changes the pronunciation of the *e* from an *eh* sound (like the middle *e* sound in "treble") to an "ay" sound.

- réveil (alarm clock)
- médecin (doctor)

The Grave Accent

The grave accent points upward and to the left, as in *è*. The grave accent can appear over the letters *a, e, i, o*, or *u*; however, it changes the pronunciation only when it appears above *e*. It's not so important in spoken French, so it can be easy to forget. The grave accent must be used in written French, however, so pay close attention to the words that use it.

- très (very)
- où (where)

The Circumflex

The circumflex, spelled *circonflexe* (sir-kohn-flex) in French, appears over vowels, like a little hat over the letter, as in *ô*. It doesn't modify the pronunciation at all, but it often indicates that an *s* used to follow the letter in Old French.

- hôtel (hotel)
- hôpital (hospital)

The Cedilla

The cedilla (in English, pronounced se-dill-ah; in French, the word is *cédille*, pronounced say-dee) appears underneath the letter *c* to make it appear like it has a tail: *ç*. It indicates a soft *s* sound instead of the hard "k" sound the letter *c* would normally have if it appeared before the letters *a*, *o*, or *u*. For example, the French language is referred to as *français*—pronounced *frahn-say*. The *c* becomes soft, turning into an "s." (If the cedilla were not present, the word would be pronounced frahn-kay.)

- garçon (boy)
- leçon (lesson)

The Umlaut

The umlaut, called *tréma* (tray-ma) in French, is the word for the two dots that appear above the second vowel when two vowels are situated together. The umlaut is used in English in some foreign words, including words borrowed from French. The accent tells you that the second vowel is to be pronounced on its own, distinct from the vowel preceding it. *Noël* and *naïve* are examples of French words that are commonly used in English; *Noël* is pronounced *no-ell*, and *naïve* is pronounced *nigh-eve*; in

French, the sound is softer and pronounced more in the front of the mouth.

- coïncidence (coincidence)
- Noël (Christmas)

Acronyms and Abbreviations

Acronyms and abbreviations can be difficult because not only do you have to know what the letters stand for, you also have to know what the spelled out words mean. Here are some common acronyms.

▶ **Common Abbreviations**

Abbreviation	Definition	English
A.R.	aller–retour	round trip
BCBG	bon chic bon genre	preppy
RSVP	répondez s'il vous plaît	please respond
TGV	train à grande vitesse	high-speed train
TTC	toutes taxes comprises	tax included
U.E.	Union européenne	EU (European Union)
W.C.	water closet	toilet

Apocopes

Apocopes, words that have one or more syllables cut off the end, are common in French. The following apocopes are considered "normal register"—you can use them when talking to anyone. Here are some informal apocopes (you should use these only with people you are on familiar terms with).

▶ Idiomatic Apocopes

Apocope	Original Word	English Word
un ado	un adolescent	teenager, adolescent
un apéro	un apéritif	cocktail before-dinner drink
un appart	un appartement	apartment, flat
cet(te) aprèm	cet(te) après-midi	this afternoon
un bac	un baccalauréat	high school diploma, A-levels
un ciné	un cinéma	movie theater
d'acc! dac!	D'accord!	OK!
déca, DK	décaféiné	decaf
un dico	un dictionnaire	dictionary
un exam	un examen	test, exam

05 / Person about Town

Survival French
Take a look at the following French phrases—they might
come in handy as you begin communication.

- I speak a little French.
- Je parle un peu de francais.
- zheu parl uh(n) peu deu fra(n)seh

- Do you speak English?
- Parlez-vous anglais?
- par lay voo a(n) gleh

- What does…mean?
- Que veut-dire…?
- keu veu deer

- How do you say…in French?
- Comment dit-on…en français?
- kuh ma(n) dee to(n)…a(n) fra(n)seh

- Repeat, please.
- Répétez, s'il vous plaît.
- ray pay tay seel voo play

- More slowly. One more time.
- Plus lentement. Encore une fois.
- plu la(n) teu ma(n); a(n) kuhr oon fwa

- I don't understand.
- Je ne comprends pas.
- zheu neu ko(n) pra(n) pa

- I don't know. What?
- Je ne sais pas. Comment?
- zheu neu say pa; kuh ma(n)

Try to speak as much French as you can before falling back on "Do you speak English?" The French will appreciate the effort you make, and the practice will make it increasingly easier for you to use your French with the next person you encounter.

Courtesy

Being polite when traveling is an absolute must. If you don't have time to learn much before you leave, at least know how to say "please" and "thank you." If you know how to be polite, you will be able to accomplish essential things like eat and find a hotel room, and you might even make some friends!

▶ **Polite Terminology**

French	Pronunciation	English
s'il vous plait	seel voo pleh	please
merci	mehr see	thank you
merci beaucoup	mehr see bo koo	thank you very much
de rien	deu ryeh(n)	you're welcome
pardon	par do(n)	pardon me
excusez-moi	eh sku zay mwa	excuse me
je suis désolé(e)	zheu swee day zuh lay	I'm sorry
à vos souhaits	a vo sweh	bless you (after a sneeze)
à votre santé	a vuh treu sa(n) tay	cheers

Nationalities and Languages

Meeting people from other countries and with different native languages is pretty much a given when you travel, and talking about where you are from is a good way to break the ice as well as an interesting way to test your knowledge of geography. The following list includes nationality adjectives in the masculine form; remember to change the to feminine endings when you need them!

▶ **Nationalities**

English	French	Pronunciation
African	africain	a free keh(n)
Algerian	algérien	al zhay ryeh(n)
(East) Asian	asiatique	a zee a teek
Australian	australien	o stra lyeh(n)
Belgian	belge	belzh
Brazilian	brésilien	bray zee lyeh(n)
Canadian	canadien	ka na dyeh(n)
Chinese	chinois	shee nwa
Dutch	néerlandais	nay eur la(n) deh
Egyptian	égyptien	ay zheep syeh(n)

English	French	Pronunciation
English	anglais	a(n) gleh
European	européen	eu ruh pay eh(n)
French	français	fra(n) seh
German	allemand	a leu ma(n)
Indian	indien	eh(n) dyeh(n)
Irish	irlandais	eer la(n) deh
Italian	italien	ee ta lyeh(n)
Japanese	japonais	zha poh neh
Mexican	mexicain	meh ksee keh(n)
Polish	polonais	poh loh neh
Portuguese	portugais	pohr tu geh
Russian	russe	rus
Spanish	espagnol	eh spa nyohl
Swiss	Suisse	swees

When these words are used as nationality adjectives, they don't need to be capitalized. However, they do need to be capitalized when used as nouns: *J'ai parlé avec un Espagnol.* (I spoke to a Spaniard.)

Getting Around and Asking for Directions

Sometimes it's fun just to wander aimlessly and discover all kinds of hidden treasures. If you're in a hurry, though, there's no shame in asking for directions.

- Where is…? It's…
- Où se trouve…? C'est…
- oo seu troov…? say…

▶ Direction

English	French	Pronunciation
north	nord	nohr
south	sud	sood
east	est	ehst
west	ouest	oo west

Places

How can you ask for directions if you don't know how to say the name of the place you're looking for? Here's some vocabulary to help you out.

▶ Places To Go

English	French	Pronunication
bank	la banque	ba(n)k
church	l'église	ay gleez
currency exchange	le bureau de change	boo ro deu sha(n)zh
hospital	l'hôpital	o pee tal
hotel	l'hôtel	o tehl
movie theater	le cinéma	see nay ma
museum	le musée	moo zay
park	le parc	park
police station	le commissariat	ko mee sa rya
post office	la poste	pohst
restaurant	le restaurant	reh sto ra(n)
school	l'école	ay kohl
theater	le théâtre	tay ahtr

Types of Transportation

The method of transportation you plan on using will determine which vocabulary is most useful to you, so figure that out first.

▶ Terms to Get You Around

English	French	Pronunciation
car	la voiture	vwa toor
taxi	le taxi	ta ksee
taxi stand	la station de taxi	sta syo(n) deu ta ksee
train	le train	tra(n)
train station	la gare	gar
bus	l'autobus	o to boos
bus stop	l'arrêt du bus	a reh doo boos
bus station	la gare routière	gar roo tyair
subway	le metro	may tro
subway station	la gare de metro	gar deu may tro
bike	un vélo	vay lo
boat	un bateau	ba to

Renting a Car

If you're staying in a large city like Paris or going from one city to another, public transportation and trains are perfect. On the other hand, if you plan to visit numerous cities and/or the countryside, renting a car can be just the thing.

- I'd like to rent a car.
- Je voudrais louer une voiture.
- zheu voo dreh loo ay oon vwa toor

▶ Rental Car Vocabulary

English	French	Pronunication
economy car	économie	ay kuh noh mee
compact car	compacte	ko(n) pakt
mid-size car	intermédiaire	e(n) tehr may dyehr
luxury car	de luxe	deu looks
convertible	décapotable	day ka poh tabl
4x4	un quatre-quatre	kat katr
truck	un camion	ka myo(n)

Here are some important questions that will allow you to seal the deal at a car rental center.

- How much will it cost?
- C'est combien?
- say ko(n) bye(n)

- Do I have to pay by the kilometer?
- Dois-je payer au kilomètre?
- dwa zheu pay ay o kee luh metr

- Is insurance included?
- L'assurance est-elle comprise?
- la su ra(s) ay tehl ko(n) preez

- I'd like to pay by credit card.
- Je voudrais payer par carte de crédit.
- zheu voo dreh pay ay par kart deu cray dee

- Where can I pick up the car?
- Où puis-je prendre la voiture?
- oo pwee zheu pra(n)dr la vwa toor

- When do I have to return it?
- Quand dois-je la rendre?
- ka(n) dwa zheu la ra(n)dr

- Can I return it to Lyon/Nice?
- Puis-je la rendre à Lyon/Nice?
- pwee zheu la ra(n)dr a lyo(n)/nees

Keep in mind that cars in Europe usually have manual transmissions. If you can't drive a stick-shift, be sure to do some calling around before you leave to find a rental company that offers cars with automatic transmission.

Airports and Hotels

Now you're ready to make your reservation, buy your ticket, and get on the plane. Here are the French phrases you'll need.

▶ Aiport Vocabulary

English	French	Pronunciation
airplane	un avion	ah vyo(n)
airport	un aéroport	ay roh por
baggage	les bagages	bah gazh
boarding pass	la carte d'embarquement	kart da(n) bar keu ma(n)
carry-on luggage	les bagages à main	bah gazh a meh(n)
cart	un chariot	sha ryo
checked luggage	les bagages enregistrés	ba gazh a(n) reu zhee stray
check-in desk	l'enregistrement	a(n) reu zhee streu ma(n)
departures	les departs	day par
early	en avance	a(n) nah vans
late	en retard	a(n) reu tar
passenger	un passager	pah sa zhay
passport	un passeport	pas por
pilot	le pilote	pee loht
shuttle	une navette	nah veht
steward	un steward	steu art
stewardess	une hôtesse de l'air	oh tehs deu lair
visa	un visa	vee zah

▶ Ticket Information

English	French	Pronunciation
flight	un vol	vohl
gate	une porte	pohrt
plane ticket	un billet d'avion	bee yay da vyo(n)
stopover	une escale	eh skal
terminal	une aérogare	a ay roh gar

▶ Travel Verbs

English	French	Pronunciation
to board	embarquer	a(n) bar kay
to buy a ticket	acheter un billet	a sheu tay uh(n) bee yay
to check bags	enregistrer (les bagages)	a(n) reu zhee stray
to sit down	s'asseoir	sa, swar
to take off	décoller	day koh lay

These verbs are in the infinitive and can be directly preceded by conjugations of the other verbs you have learned. For example, *Je voudrais acheter un billet.* (I'd like to buy a ticket.) *Nous allons embarquer.* (We're going to board.)

Baggage Claim, Immigration, and Customs

Once you've arrived at your destination, you need to collect your luggage and go through immigration and customs. Here is the vocabulary you may need.

Useful Phrases

- Mes bagages sont égarés. (My luggage is missing.)
- Voici mon passeport. (Here's my passport.)
- J'ai un visa. (I have a visa.)
- Je voudrais declarer. . . (I would like to declare. . .)

Get a Room!

You made it! After your flight and airport negotiations, you're probably ready to take a nap before going out to explore the town. Here are some words and phrases for getting the accommodations you want.

In some inexpensive French hotels, the bathroom is often down the hall. If you want a toilet/sink/shower in your room, you need to make that clear when reserving your room.

You will often start with this phrase, "I would like a room for/with…" or *Je voudrais une chambre pour/ avec…* (zheu voo dreh oon sha(n)br poor/a vehk).

▶ **Hotel Vocabulary**

English	French	Pronunciation
one night	une nuit	oon nwee
two people	deux personnes	deu pehr sohn
two beds	deux lits	deu lee
a double bed	un grand lit	u(n) gra(n) lee
a toilet	des toilettes	day twa leht
a television	une télévision	oon tay lay vee zyo(n)
a telephone	un téléphone	u(n) tay lay fuhn
air conditioning	la climatisation	la klee ma tee zah syo(n)

You may also want to say "Do you have/Is there…?" or *Avez-vous/Est-ce qu'il y a…?* (a vay voo/es keel ee a):

Here are some things that you may want to be able to stay while you are staying at the hotel.

- I would like a wake-up call at 8 a.m.
- Je voudrais être réveillé à huit heures.
- zheu voo dreh eht ray vay ay a weet eur

- What is the check-out time?
- Il faut libérer la chambre à quelle heure?
- eel fo lee bay ray la sha(n)br a kel leur

- How much is it?
- C'est combien?
- say co(n) bye(n)

- I would like to pay my bill.
- Je voudrais régler mon compte.
- zheu voo dreh ray glay mo(n) co(n)t

- The bill is incorrect.
- L'addition n'est pas correcte.
- la dee syo(n) nay pa kuh rehkt

- I would like to pay…
- Je voudrais payer…
- zheu voo dreh pay ay

▶ Ways You Can Pay

English	French	Pronunciation
in cash	en espèces	a(n) eh spehs
with traveler's checks	avec des chèques de voyage	a vehk day shehk deu vwa yazh
with a credit card	avec une carte de credit	a veh koon kart deu kray dee

In Case of an Emergency

Hopefully you won't ever need to know French emergency vocabulary, but here's some just in case you do:

▶ Emergency Vocabulary

English	French	Pronunciation
Emergency!	Urgence!	oor zha(n)s
Help!	Au secours!	o seu koor
Fire!	Au feu!	o feu
Police!	Police!	puh lees
Thief!	Au voleur!	o vuh leur
Watch out!	Attention!	a ta(n) syo(n)
accident	un accident	a ksee da(n)
attack	une attaque	a tak
burglary	un cambriolage	ka(n) bree yuh lazh
crash	une collision	kuh lee zyo(n)
explosion	une explosion	ehk spluh zyo(n)
flood	une inondation	ee no(n) da syo(n)
gunshot	un coup de feu	koo deu feu
mugging	une aggression	a greh syo(n)
rape	un viol	vyul
theft	un vol	vul
to need	avoir besoin de / d'	a vwar beu zwa(n) deu
ambulance	une ambulance	a(n) boo la(n)s
doctor	un médecin	may deu seh(n)
fireman	un pompier	po(n) pyay
to be drowning	se noyer	seu nwa yay
to be in labor	être en train d'accoucher	etr a(n) tra(n) da koo shay

Common French Phrases

This last section provides lists of common French expressions organized by verb. Some of these expressions can be more or less literally translated into English; those that cannot be literally translated are known as idiomatic expressions and are understandably more difficult to learn and remember. But you'll start to recognize these because most of them are very common.

Expressions with *Aller*

The French verb *aller* means "to go" and is an irregular verb.

▶ **Expressions with *Aller***

English	French
to be going to	aller + infinitive
to go fishing	aller à la pêche
to go meet someone	aller rencontrer quelqu'un
to go on foot	aller à pied
to be becoming, to suit	aller à quelqu'un
to go meet someone	aller au-devant de quelqu'un
to get to the bottom of things	aller au fond des choses
to match something	aller avec quelque chose
to get, to fetch	aller chercher
to go hand in hand with	aller de pair avec
to ride in a car	aller en voiture
Go ahead!	Allez-y!
Come on then.	Allons donc!
Let's go!	Allons-y!
How are you?	Ça va?
That goes without saying.	Ça va sans dire
How are you?	Comment allez-vous?
How are you?	Comment vas-tu?
Shall we go?	On y va?
to go away	s'en aller

If you need to tell someone to go away, *s'en aller* becomes *va-t-en*! On the other hand, if you want to tell someone that you'll go away (and leave them alone), say *je m'en vais*. The conjugations are pretty tricky, but these are probably the only two you'll need.

Expressions with Donner

The verb *donner* means "to give." There are several commonly used expressions that use this verb.

▶ Expressions with *Donner*

English	French
to guess that someone is . . . years old	donner . . . ans à quelqu'un
to be on full-blast (e.g., radio, TV)	donner à fond, à plein
to make someone think that	donner à quelqu'un à penser que
to face north/south	donner au nord/sud
to give someone an appetite	donner de l'appétit à quelqu'un
to make someone feel hungry/cold	donner faim/froid à quelqu'un
to make someone seasick	donner le mal de mer à quelqu'un
to make someone feel dizzy	donner le vertige à quelqu'un
to tell someone the time	donner l'heure à quelqu'un
to order someone to + verb	donner l'ordre à quelqu'un de + infinitive
to take something in to be repaired	donner quelque chose à (+ a business)
to give someone something to do	donner quelque chose à faire à quelqu'un
to trade, swap	donner quelque chose contre quelque chose
to give up one's seat	donner sa place
to offer one's friendship to someone	donner son amitié à quelqu'un
to give one's heart to someone	donner son cœur à quelqu'un
to give someone a kiss	donner un baiser à quelqu'un
to give someone a call	donner un coup de fil à quelqu'un
to help someone out	donner un coup de main à quelqu'un (informal)
to sweep/dust quickly	donner un coup de balai/chiffon

You might think that *donner* doesn't have anything to do with English, but in fact it shares an etymological root with the word "donate."

Expressions with Faire

In addition to the uses of *faire* (to do, make) with weather, sports, and musical instruments discussed elsewhere in this book, the verb *faire* is used in many common French expressions.

▶ **Expressions with *Faire***

English	French
to welcome	faire bon accueil
to run errands/to go shopping	faire les courses
to do homework	faire ses devoirs
to take a walk (a ride)	faire une promenade
to pay a visit	faire une visite
to take a trip	faire un voyage

Faire followed by a verb means "to make something happen" or "to have something done":

■ Le froid fait geler l'eau.
■ Cold makes water freeze.

■ Je fais laver la voiture.
■ I'm having the car washed.

Faire une promenade and *faire un tour* both mean "to take a walk," whereas the addition of *en voiture* to either expression changes it to mean "to take a ride."

Expressions with Mettre

Mettre literally means "to put" and is an irregular verb: *je mets, tu mets, il met, nous mettons, vous mettez, ils mettent.*

▶ Expressions with *Mettre*

English	French
to put money into	mettre de l'argent dans
to spend money on	mettre de l'argent sur
to turn on the radio	mettre la radio
to bring out, enhance	mettre en relief
to set the alarm	mettre le réveil
to bring someone in line	mettre quelqu'un au pas

Expressions with Rendre

Rendre means "to give something back" or "to return something." With an adjective, it means "to make something" + that adjective, such as *rendre heureux* (to make happy).

▶ Expressions with *Rendre*

English	French
to breathe one's last	rendre l'âme
to worship	rendre un culte à
to glorify	rendre gloire à
to pay homage to	rendre hommage à
to pay tribute to	rendre honneur à
to visit someone	rendre visite à quelqu'un

Impersonal Expressions

Impersonal expressions are those that do not have a specific subject. In French, the impersonal subject is expressed with either *il* or *ce*. The expressions listed here can be followed by either *de* + infinitive or *que* + subject + conjugated verb:

- Il est important d'étudier
- It's important to study.

- Il est probable que David étudie.
- David is probably studying.

▶ Impersonal Expressions

English	French
English	*French*
It's amazing	Il est étonnant
It's certain	Il est certain
It's doubtful	Il est douteux
It's good	Il est bon
It's important	Il est important
It's impossible	Il est impossible
It's improbable	Il est improbable
It's necessary	Il est nécessaire
It's normal	Il est normal
It's obvious	Il est évident
It's possible	Il est possible
It's probable	Il est probable
It's rare	Il est rare
It's regrettable	Il est regrettable
It's shameful	Il est honteux
It's sure/certain	Il est sûr/certain
It's time	Il est temps
It's true	Il est vrai
It's useful	Il est utile
It's useless	Il est inutile

Appendix A / French–English Dictionary

A

à bientôt	see you soon
à côté de	next to
à demain	see you tomorrow
à deux lits	with two beds
à droite	right
à gauche	left
à la carte	side order (not part of "le menu")
à la prochaine	until next time
à point	medium-rare
à tout à l'heure	see you soon
à vos / tes souhaits	bless you (after a sneeze)
à votre / ta santé	cheers
un abricot	apricot
un accélérateur	gas pedal
un accident	accident
acheter	to buy
un acteur	actor
une actrice	actress
l'addition	check, bill
adieu	farewell
une adresse	address
une aérogare	terminal
un aéroport	airport
une affiche	poster
l'agneau	lamb
une agrafe	staple
une agrafeuse	stapler
aller	to go
allergique à	allergic to

Allez-y!	Go ahead!
Allô?	Hello?
Allons donc!	Come on then.
Allons-y!	Let's go!
l'amande	almond
un(e) amante	lover
une ambulance	ambulance
aimable	friendly
un(e) ami(e)	friend
les anchois	anchovies
une anesthésie locale	local anesthesia
les animaux sont interdits	no pets allowed
l'anniversaire de mariage	wedding anniversary
un annuaire	phone book
un anorak	ski jacket
un apéritif	cocktail
un appel en P.C.V.	collect call
appeler	to call
l'arachide	peanut
l'argent	money
une armoire	closet
arracher	to pull out, remove
l'arrêt du bus	bus stop
l'arthrite	arthritis
les arrivées	arrivals
un(e) artiste	artist
un ascenseur	elevator
les asperges	asparagus
l'aspirine	aspirin
une assiette	plate
l'assistance	help
assuré	confident, insured
asthmatique	asthmatic
Attention!	Watch out!

atterrir	to land
Au feu!	Fire!
Au revoir	Good-bye
Au secours!	Help!
Au voleur!	Thief!
une aubergine	eggplant
une auto	car
l'autobus	bus
automne	autumn
une autoroute	highway
autres destinations	other destinations
avec	with
Avez-vous un(e) ...?	Do you have a(n) ...?
un avion	airplane
l'avis de réception	return receipt
un(e) avocat(e)	lawyer, barrister
avoir	to have

B

le babeurre	buttermilk
les bagages	baggage
les bagages à main	carry-on luggage
les bagages enregistrés	checked luggage
une bague	ring
une bague de fiançailles	engagement ring
une baguette	French bread
la baignoire	bathtub
le bain	bath
le bain moussant	bubble bath
le balcon	balcony
une banane	banana
une banque	bank
une barrette	barrette
des bas	stockings
le base-ball	baseball

la base (de maquillage)	foundation (makeup)
le basket(-ball)	basketball
un bateau	boat
le baume démêlant	hair conditioner
beau	handsome
Il fait beau	It's nice weather
belle	beautiful
le beurre	butter
une bicyclette	bicycle
bien cuit	well done (meat)
la bière	beer
le bifteck	steak
des bijoux	jewelry
un bikini	bikini
un billet	paper money, note, bill, ticket
un billet aller-retour	round trip ticket
le billet d'avion	plane ticket
un billet aller	one-way ticket
le biscuit	cookie
blanc	white
la blanchisserie	laundromat
le blé	wheat
bleu	blue; rare (meat)
blond(e)	blond
un blouson	jacket
boire	to drink
une boîte	can, box, tin
une boîte aux lettres	mailbox
un bol	bowl
bon appétit!	Enjoy your meal
les bonbons	candy
Bonjour	Hello
Bonne nuit	Good night
Bonsoir	Good evening

des bottes	boots
la bouche	mouth
un boucher	butcher
la boucherie	butcher shop
bouclé	curly
une boucle d'oreille	earring
un boulanger (une boulangère)	baker
la boulangerie	bakery
une bouteille	bottle
une boutique hors taxes	duty-free shop
un bouton de manchette	cufflink
la boxe	boxing
un bracelet	bracelet
le bras	arm
bronzé	tanned
le brouillard	fog
des brûlures d'estomac	heartburn
brune	brown (hair)
un bureau	desk, office, study
un bureau de change	currency exchange

C

une cabine téléphonique	phone booth
la cacahuète	peanut
un cache-nez	muffler
un cadeau	present
le café	coffee
un café	café
un cahier	notebook
un caissier (une caissière)	cashier
une calculatrice	calculator
un caleçon	boxer shorts
un camion	truck
le canapé	sofa, couch

un carnet de chèques	checkbook
un carnet de timbres	book of stamps
la carte	menu, map
une carte bancaire	ATM/bank card
une carte de crédit	credit card
la carte d'embarquement	boarding pass
une carte postale	post card
se casser le bras/a jambe	to break one's arm/leg
une casserole	baking dish
une ceinture	belt, cummerbund
le céleri	celery
une cerise	cherry
C'est . . . à l'appareil.	. . . is calling.
C'est combien?	How much is it?
C'est . . .	It's . . .
une chaîne stéréo	stereo
une chaise	chair
un châle	shawl
la chambre	bedroom, hotel room
le champignon	mushroom
le changement d'adresse	change of address
changer de l'argent	to change money
un chapeau	hat
la charcuterie	pork butcher, deli
un chariot	cart
un charpentier	carpenter
la chasse	hunting
chasser	to hunt
chaud	hot
des chaussettes	socks
des chaussures	shoes
un chef	boss, manager
un(e) chef	cook
une chemise	file folder; men's shirt, blouse

une chemise de nuit	nightgown
un chèque	check, cheque
un chèque certifié	certified check
un chèque de voyage	traveler's check
les cheveux	hair
la cheville	ankle
chez le dentiste	at the dentist's office
chez moi	at my house
le chocolat	chocolate
le chocolat chaud	hot chocolate
le chou-fleur	cauliflower
Chronopost	Express mail
le cinéma	movie theater
cinq	five
cinquante	fifty
circuler	to go, move
un citron	lemon
le citron pressé	lemonade
un citron vert	lime
la classe touriste	coach, economy class
le clignotant	turn signal
un colis	package
un collant	pantyhose, tights
un collège	junior high school
un collier	necklace
une collision	crash
une combinaison	slip
Combien coûte . . . ?	How much does . . . cost?
commander	to order
comme ci, comme ça	so-so
comment	how
Comment?	What?
le commissariat	police station
une commode	dresser

une compagnie aérienne	airline
une copine	girlfriend
complet	no vacancy
composer un numéro	to dial a number
un compte chèque postal (CCP)	postal checking account
un compte d'épargne	savings account
un compte-chèques	checking account
compter	to count
le concombre	cucumber
un conducteur	driver
conduire	to drive
la confiserie	candy store
la confiture	jam
confus	embarassed
constipé	constipated
un contrat	contract
le contrôle de sécurité	security check
un copain	boyfriend
un costume	suit (man's)
le cou	neck
le coude	elbow
le couloir	hall
un coup de feu	gunshot
un coup de soleil	sunburn
courageuse	brave
la couronne	crown
le courriel	email
le courrier	(postal) mail
un cours	course
court	short (length)
un(e) cousin(e)	cousin
un couteau	knife
une craie	chalk
une cravate	tie

un crayon	pencil
la crème	cream
la crème à raser	shaving cream
la crème brûlée	custard
la crème caramel	flan
la crème fraîche	very thick cream
la crème hydratante	moisturizer
un croissant	croissant
une cuiller à mesurer	measuring spoon
une cuiller	spoon
une cuillère à soupe	tablespoon
une cuillère à thé	teaspoon
la cuisine	cooking, kitchen
cuisiner	to cook
une cuisinière	stove
une culotte	panties
le cyclisme	biking

D

d'accord	OK
la danse	dance, dancing
danser	to dance
de rien	you're welcome
déclarer	to declare
décoller	to take off
décrocher	to pick up (the phone)
défense de fumer	no smoking
définitif/ve	permanent
le déjeuner	lunch
un(e) dentiste	dentist
le déodorant	deodorant
les départs	departures
dépenser	to spend
déposer	to deposit
désolé(e)	sorry

désorienté	confused
le dessert	dessert
le destinataire	recipient
le détartrage	teeth cleaning
la dévitalisation	root canal
des devoirs	homework
diabétique	diabetic
la diarrhée	diarrhea
un dictionnaire	dictionary
le digestif	after-dinner drink
la dimension	size (of a package)
la dinde	turkey
le dîner	dinner
le directeur général	CEO
le dissolvant	nail polish remover
le doigt	finger
le dos	back
la douane	customs
doublé	dubbed
doubler	to pass
la douche	shower
douze	twelve
la droguerie	drugstore
drôle	funny

E

l'eau (f)	water
l'eau dentifrice	mouthwash
les échecs	chess
une école	school
écouter (de) la musique	to listen to music
un écrivain	writer
effrayé	scared
l'église (f)	church
un électricien	electrician

elle	she
embarquer	to board
embaucher	to hire
un embouteillage	traffic jam
un(e) employé(e)	employee
un emprunt	loan
en arrière de	in back of
en avance	early
en avant de	in front of
en bas	down
en classe touriste	in economy class
en haut	up
en panne	broken-down
en première classe	in first class
en retard	late
en route	on the way
enceinte	pregnant
enchanté	pleased to meet you
encore une fois	one more time
des engelures	frostbite
ennuyé	annoyed, bored
ennuyeux/ennuyeuse	boring
l'enregistrement	check-in
enregistrer (les bagages)	to check bags
enrhumé	cold (illness)
une enveloppe	envelope
une épaule	shoulder
l'épicerie	grocery store
les épinards	spinach
une épingle	pin
épuisé/épuisée	exhausted
une escale	stopover
un escalier	stairway
les escargots	snails

des espèces	cash
l'essence (f)	gas, petrol
essence ordinaire	regular gas
les essuie-glaces	windshield wipers
est	east
un estomac	stomach
et	and
une étagère	bookshelf
l'été	summer
éternuer	to sneeze
être	to be
un(e) étudiant(e)	student
s'évanouir	to faint
un évier	sink (kitchen)
un examen	test
excité	hyper(active)
une excursion	trip
excusez-moi	excuse me
l'expéditeur	sender
une explosion	explosion
un expresso	espresso

F

fâché/fâchée	angry
faible	weak
faire	to do, make
le fard à joues	blusher (cosmetic)
le fard à paupières	eyeshadow
fatigué/fatiguée	tired
fatiguée dû au décalage horaire	jet lagged
une femme	woman, wife
une femme de chambre	maid
une fenêtre	window
un feu	fire

le feu rouge	stop light
les feux de route	high beams
les feux de stop	brake lights
une feuille de papier	sheet of paper
les fiançailles	engagement
un(e) fiancé(e)	fiance(e)
se fiancer	to get engaged
la fièvre	fever
un fils	son
fne fleur	flower
la flûte	flute; thin French bread
un(e) fonctionnaire	civil servant
le foot(ball)	soccer
le football américain	football (US)
fort/forte	strong
des fossettes	dimples
un foulard	scarf
un four	oven
un four à micro-ondes	microwave oven
une fourchette	fork
frais	cool
les frais	fees
les freins	brakes
un frère	brother
les frites	fries
Il fait froid/froid/froide	It's cold (weather)
le fromage	cheese
le fromage blanc	cream cheese
les fruits	fruit

G

gagner	to earn
des gants (m)	gloves
un gant de cuisine	oven mitt
un garçon	boy

la gare	train station
la gare de métro	subway station
garer (la voiture)	to park
la gare routière	bus station
le gâteau	cake
geler	freeze
la gencive	gum
le genou	knee
gentil/gentille	kind
un gérant	manager
la glace	ice cream
le golf	golf
une gomme	eraser
le goûter	snack
grand/grande	tall
le grand magasin	department store
une grand-mère	grandmother
un grand-père	grandfather
le grenier	attic
un grille-pain	toaster
la grippe	flu
gris/grise	grey
gros/grosse	fat
le guichet	counter, window
un guichet automatique	ATM machine
la guitare	guitar

H

un haricot	bean
des hémorroïdes	hemorrhoids
heureux/heureuse	happy
l'hiver (m)	winter
le hockey	hockey
un homme	man
honteux/honteuse	ashamed

l'hôpital (m)	hospital
l'hôtel (m)	hotel
une hôtesse de l'air	stewardess
huit	eight
humide	humid

I

il	he, it
il y a	there is, there are
l'immigration (f)	immigration
impatient/ impatiente	impatient
un imperméable	raincoat
une imprimante	printer
l'imprimé	form
infecté	infected
un infirmier (une infirmière)	nurse
un ingénieur	engineer
une inondation	flood
inquiet/inquiéte	worried
insomniaque	insomniac
intelligent/intelligente	smart
intéressant	interesting
l'iode	iodine

J

la jambe	leg
le jambon	ham
le jardin	garden, yard
jardiner	to garden
jaune	yellow
un jean	jeans
le jogging	jogging
joli	good-looking
jolie	pretty
la joue	cheek

jouer à	to play (game, sport)
jouer de	to play (music)
un journal	newspaper
une jupe	skirt
un jupon	half slip
le jus	juice

K, L

un kilogramme (un kilo)	kilogram
un kiosque	newsstand
lâche	cowardly
laid/laide	ugly
laisser un message	to leave a message
le lait	milk
la laitue	lettuce
une lampe	lamp
le lapin	rabbit
le lavabo	sink (bathroom)
se laver	to wash (oneself)
un lave-vaisselle	dishwasher
la lecture	reading
une lettre	letter
la lèvre	lip
licencier	to lay off
la lime à ongles	nail file
lire	to read
un lit	bed
un litre	liter
un livre	book
une livre	pound
le logement	accommodations
loin (de)	far (from)
long	long
lourd/lourde	heavy
la lune de miel	honeymoon

des lunettes	eyeglasses
des lunettes de soleil	sunglasses
la lutte	wrestling
lutter	to wrestle, to fight
un lycée	high school

M

la mâchoire	jaw
Madame	Ma'am, Mrs.
Mademoiselle	Miss
la main	hand
la maison	house
un magasin	store
le magasin de confection	clothing store
un magazine	magazine
un maillot (de bain)	bathing suit
un maillot de corps	undershirt
le maïs	corn
le mal de mer	seasickness
malade	sick
le mandat	money order
manger	to eat
un manteau	coat
le maquillage	makeup (cosmetic)
se maquiller	to put on makeup
le marché	outdoor market
un mari	husband
le mariage	wedding
se marier avec	to get married
une marmite	pot
marron	brown
le mascara	mascara
mauvais/mauvaire	bad
Il fait mauvais.	It's bad weather.
la mayonnaise	mayonnaise

un mécanicien	mechanic
méchant/méchante	mean
un médecin	doctor
le menu	fixed-price meal
merci (bien/beaucoup)	thank you (very much)
une mère	mother
le métro	subway
mille fois merci	bless you! (thank you so much)
un mille	mile
un milliard	billion
mince	thin
une minijupe	miniskirt
un miroir	mirror
un mobile	cell phone
une mobylette	moped
moche	ugly
la molaire	molar
la monnaie	change
Monsieur	Mr., Sir
le montant	amount, total, sum
une montre	watch
une moto	motorcycle
un mouchoir	handkerchief
des moufles (f)	mittens
la mousse au chocolat	chocolate mousse
la moutarde	mustard
un mur	wall
le musée	museum
la musique	music

N

nager	to swim
naïf	naive
la natation	swimming
une navette	shuttle

navré	sorry, distressed
ne . . . pas	not
neige	snow
neiger	to snow (verb)
nerveux/nerveuse	nervous
neuf	nine, new
un neveu	nephew
le nez	nose
une nièce	niece
les noces (f)	wedding
noir	black
noisette	hazelnut
non	no
nord	north
un noeud papillon	bow tie
la Novocaïne	Novocain
se noyer	to be drowning
nuageux/nuageuse	cloudy
un numéro de téléphone	phone number

O

un oeil (des yeux)	eye(s)
l'oeuf (m)	egg
un oignon	onion
un oncle	uncle
ondulé/ondulée	wavy
un ongle	fingernail
onze	eleven
l'opéra (m)	opera
orageux/orageuse	stormy
orange	orange (color)
une orange	orange
l'orchestre (m)	orchestra
un ordinateur	computer
une oreille	ear

un oreiller	pillow
un orteil	toe
ou	or
où	where
Où est . . .?	Where is . . .?
ouest	west
oui	yes
ouvert/ouverte	outgoing, open
ouvrez la bouche	open your mouth

P

le pain	bread
le pain complet	wholegrain bread
le pain de seigle	rye bread
un pamplemousse	grapefruit
un pantalon	pants
le papier	paper
un paquet	package
par avion	air mail
par express	special delivery
un parapluie	umbrella
le parc	park
pardon	pardon me
paresseux/paresseuse	lazy
le parfum	perfume
le parking	parking lot/garage
un passager	passenger
un passeport	passport
les pâtes	pasta
patient/patiente	patient
le patio	patio
la pâtisserie	pastry shop
patriotique	patriotic
payer	to pay
un péage	toll

une pêche	peach
la pêche	fishing
pêcher	to fish
le peigne	comb
une peinture	painting
un pendentif	pendant
la pénicilline	penicillin
perdre	to lose
un père	father
petit/petite	short (height)
le petit-déjeuner	breakfast
une petite annonce	classified ad
une petit-fille	granddaughter
un petit-fils	grandson
les petits pois	peas
la pharmacie	pharmacy
un(e) pharmacien(ne)	pharmacist
les phares (m)	headlights
le piano	piano
la pièce	room
une pièce (de monnaie)	coin
un pied	foot
le pilote	pilot
une piqûre	injection
la piscine	pool
un placard	closet
la place	seat
le plafond	ceiling
une planche à découper	cutting board
le plat principal	main course
un plombage	filling
un plombier	plumber
la plongée	diving
plus	more, very

le poids	weight
le poignet	wrist
une poire	pear
le poisson	fish
la poissonnerie	fish store
la poitrine	chest
le poivre	pepper
un policier	police officer
un pompier	fireman
le porc	pork
le porche	porch
une porte	door, gate
un porte-documents	briefcase
un portefeuille	wallet
la poste	post office
la poste restante	general delivery, hold mail
un pot	cup, jar
le potage	soup
le pouce	thumb, inch
le poulet	chicken
pour	for
le pourboire	tip
pourquoi	why
la première classe	first class
le premier étage	second floor (US)
près (de)	near (to)
pressé/pressée	rushed, in a hurry
le printemps	spring
le prix	price
les produits laitiers	dairy products
un professeur	teacher
provisoire	temporary
une prune	plum
les P.T.T.	post office

un pull	sweater
un pupitre	student desk
un pyjama	pajamas

Q, R

le quai	platform
quand	when
quarante	forty
quatorze	fourteen
quatre	four
qui	who
quinze	fifteen
quoi	what
raccrocher	to hang up
le radis	radish
raffiné/raffinée	sophisticated
raide	straight (hair)
un raisin	grape
la randonnée	hiking
rappeler	to call back
le rasage	shaving
se raser	to shave
le rasoir	razor
le rasoir électrique	shaver
ravi/ravie	delighted
la réception des bagages	baggage claim
un(e) réceptionniste	receptionist
une recette	recipe
recommandé	registered (mail)
un reçu	receipt
la réexpédition	forwarding
un réfrigérateur	refrigerator
regarder la télé	to watch TV
regarder un film	to watch a movie
régler le compte	to pay the bill

un relevé de compte	bank statement
remplacer	to replace
le rendement	yield
renvoyer	to return; to fire (an employee)
le repas	meal
un répondeur téléphonique	answering machine
un responsable	manager
le restaurant	restaurant
retirer	to withdraw
un réveil	alarm clock
le rez-de-chaussée	first floor (US)
un rhume des foins	hay fever
un rideau	curtain
rien	nothing
rincer	to rinse
le riz	rice
une robe	dress
le rosbif	roast beef
rose	pink
une rose	rose
rouge	red
le rouge à lèvres	lipstick
un rouleau à pâtisserie	rolling pin
rouler	to drive
roux, rousse	red (hair)
un ruban	ribbon
la rue	street
russe	Russian

S

un sac à dos	backpack
un sac à main	purse
saigner	to bleed
les saisons (f)	seasons
la salade	salad

la salle	room
la salle à manger	dining room
la salle de bains	bathroom
une salle de classe	classroom
la salle de séjour	den
le salon	living room
salut	hi, bye
des sandales	sandals
sans préjugés	open-minded
le saucisson	sausage
le savon	soap
le saxophone	saxophone
la séance	showing, time
un(e) secrétaire	secretary
seize	sixteen
le sel	salt
sept	seven
sérieux/sérieuse	serious
un serveur	waiter
une serveuse	waitress
service compris	tip included
le service de lessive	laundry service
service non compris	tip not included
une serviette	napkin, towel
le shampooing	shampoo
un short	shorts
si	yes
signer	to sign
s'il vous/te plaît	please
la sinusite	sinusitis
six	six
le skate	skateboarding
le ski	skiing
un smoking	tuxedo

snob	snobbish
une soeur	sister
soixante	sixty
soixante-dix	seventy
le sol	floor
le solde	balance
du soleil	sunny
solitaire	lonely
sonner	to ring
sortir avec	to date
une soucoupe	saucer
la soupe	soup
le sous-sol	basement
un soutien-gorge	bra
sous-titré	subtitled
sous-vêtements (m)	underwear
un spectacle	show, performance
sportif/sportive	athletic
la station de métro	subway station
la station de taxi	taxi stand
stationner	to park
une station-service	gas station
un steward	steward
studieux/studieuse	studious
stupide	stupid
un stylo	pen
le sucre	sugar
sud	south
un surligneur	highlighter
sympathique (sympa)	nice
la symphonie	symphony

T, U

un tabac	tobacco store
une table	table

un tableau	chalkboard
des taches de rousseur (f)	freckles
un tailleur	suit (woman's)
une tante	aunt
un tapis	rug
taquin	playful
la tarte	pie
une tasse	cup
le taux de change	exchange rate
le taux d'intérêt	interest rate
la télé	TV
un téléphone	telephone
téléphoner à	to call (phone)
la télévision	television
le tennis	tennis
des tennis	sneakers
la tension artérielle	blood pressure
la tête	head
le thé	tea
le théâtre	theater
un timbre	stamp
timbres en gros (m)	bulk stamps
timide	shy
le tir à l'arc	archery
la toilette	toilet
les toilettes	restroom
la tomate	tomato
la tonalité	dial tone
un torchon	dish towel
toucher un chèque	to cash a check
tourner	to turn
tousser	to cough
tout droit	straight ahead
le train	train

tranquille	calm
une transmission automatique	automatic transmission
le transport	transportation
travailler	to work
travailleur	hard-working
traverser	to cross
triste	sad
une trombone	paper clip
une université	college, university
Urgence!	Emergency!

V, Y

la vanille	vanilla
le veau	veal
végétarien(ne)	vegetarian
un vélo	bike
vendre	to sell
un verre	glass
un verre gradué	measuring cup
vert/verte	green
le vertige	dizziness
des vêtements (m)	clothes
veuillez (in front of a verb)	please
le vin	wine
un visa	visa
le visage	face
la voile	sailing
violet	purple
voici	this is
une voiture	car
un vol	flight, theft
vomir	to throw up
vouloir	to want
le yaourt	yogurt
les yeux (un oeil)	eyes (eye)

Appendix B / English–French Dictionary

A

accident	un accident
accommodations	le logement
to ache all over	avoir mal partout
actor	un acteur
actress	une actrice
adding machine	une machine à calculer
address	une adresse
after-dinner drink	le digestif
air conditioner	un climatiseur
air mail	par avion
airline	une compagnie aérienne
airplane	un avion
airport	un aéroport
alarm clock	un réveil
allergic to	allergique à
amount, total, sum	le montant
ambulance	une ambulance
and	et
angry	fâché(e)
ankle	la cheville
anniversary	l'anniversaire
annoyed	ennuyé(e)
answering machine	un répondeur téléphonique
appetizers	les hors-d'oeuvre (m)
archery	le tir à l'arc
arm	le bras
arrivals	les arrivées
artist	un(e) artiste
ashamed	honteux/honteuse

aspirin	une aspirine
asthmatic	asthmatique
athletic	sportif/sportive
ATM card	une carte bancaire
ATM machine	un guichet automatique
attic	le grenier
aunt	une tante
automatic transmission	une transmission automatique
autumn	l'automne

B

back	le dos
backpack	un sac à dos
bad	mal, mauvais/mauvaise
bad weather	mauvais temps
baggage	les bagages (m)
baggage claim	la réception des bagages
baker	un boulanger/une boulangère
bakery	la boulangerie
baking dish	une casserole
balance	le solde
bank	une banque
bank card	une carte bancaire
barber	le coiffeur
baseball	le base-ball
basement	le sous-sol
basketball	le basket(-ball)
bathing suit	un maillot (de bain)
bathroom	la salle de bains
to be	être
bean	un haricot
bed	un lit
bedroom	la chambre
beer	la bière
belt	une ceinture
bicycle; bike	une bicyclette; un vélo

biking	le cyclisme
bikini	un bikini
bill	l'addition (f)
binder	un classeur
black	noir
to bleed	saigner
bless you (after a sneeze)	à vos/tes souhaits
blond	blond(e)
blood pressure	la tension artérielle
blue	bleu
to blunder	faire une gaffe
blusher	le fard à joues
to board	embarquer
boarding pass	la carte d'embarquement
boat	un bateau
to bolt the door	mettre le verrou
book	un livre
bookshelf	une étagère
boots	des bottes (f)
bored	ennuyé/ennuyée
boss	le chef
bottle	une bouteille
boxing	la boxe
boy	un garçon
boyfriend	un copain
bra	un soutien-gorge
brakes	les freins (m)
brave	courageux/courageuse
bread	le pain
to break (arm, leg)	se casser (le bras, la jambe)
breakfast	le petit-déjeuner
brother	un frère
brown	marron
brown (hair)	brun/brune

to brush one's hair	se brosser les cheveux
to brush one's teeth	se brosser les dents
bubble bath	le bain moussant
bulk stamps	timbres en gros
bus	l'autobus
bus station	la gare routière
bus stop	l'arrêt du bus
busy	occupé/occupée
butcher	un boucher
butter	le beurre
to buy	acheter
bye	salut

C

cake	le gâteau
calculator	une calculatrice
to call	appeler, téléphoner à
to call back	rappeler
calm	tranquille
can, box, tin	une boîte
candy	des bonbons (m)
candy store	la confiserie
car	une auto, une voiture
carpenter	un charpentier
carpet	une moquette
carrot	la carotte
carry-on luggage	les bagages à main
cart	un chariot
cash	des espèces
to cash a check	encaisser, toucher un chèque
cash dispenser	un guichet automatique bancaire (GAB)
cashier	un caissier (une caissière)
cell phone	un mobile
certified check	un chèque certifié
chair	une chaise

chalk	une craie
chalkboard	un tableau
change	la monnaie
to change money	changer de l'argent (en Euros)
check, bill	l'addition (f)
to check bags	enregistrer (les bagages)
checkbook	un carnet de chèques
checked luggage	les bagages enregistrés
check-in	l'enregistrement (m)
checking account	un compte-chèques
cheek	la joue
cheers	à votre/ta santé
cheese	le fromage
chess	les échecs
chest	la poitrine
chicken	le poulet
chocolate	le chocolat
church	l'église (f)
classroom	une salle de classe
closet	une armoire, un placard
clothes	des vêtements
clothing store	le magasin de confection
cloudy	nuageux/nuageuse
coach class	la classe touriste
coat	un manteau
cocktail	un apéritif
coffee	le café
coin	une pièce (de monnaie)
cold (illness)	un rhume
cold (temperature)	froid/froide
collect call	un appel en P.C.V.
college	une université
comb	le peigne
compact car	une voiture compacte

to compel	mettre dans l'obligation de
computer	un ordinateur
conditioner (hair)	le baume démêlant
confident	assuré/assurée
confused	désorienté/désorientée
constipated	constipé/constipée
contract	un contrat
convertible (car)	une voiture décapotable
cook	le/la chef
to cook	cuisiner, faire la cuisine
cookbook	un livre de cuisine
cookie	le biscuit
cooking	la cuisine
cool	frais
corn	le maïs
couch	un canapé
to cough	tousser
to count	compter
course	un cours
cousin	un(e) cousin(e)
crash	une collision
cream	la crème
credit card	une carte de crédit
cup	une tasse
curly	bouclé/bouclée
currency exchange	un bureau de change
curtain	un rideau
custard	la crème brûlée
customs	la douane
cutting board	une planche à découper

D

dairy products	les produits laitiers
dance, dancing	la danse
to dance	danser

dark blue	bleu foncé
to date	sortir avec
to declare	déclarer
delighted	ravi/ravie
den	la salle de séjour
deodorant	le déodorant
department store	le grand magasin
departures	les départs
to deposit (into an account)	déposer (sur un compte)
desk	un bureau, un pupitre
dessert	le dessert
diabetic	diabétique
dial tone	la tonalité
diarrhea	la diarrhée
dictionary	un dictionnaire
dimples	des fossettes
dining room	la salle à manger
dinner	le dîner
dishwasher	un lave-vaisselle
distressed, sorry	navré/navrée
dizzy	le vertige
to do, make	faire
doctor	un médecin
don't mention it	il n'y a pas de quoi
door	une porte
double bed	un grand lit
down	en bas
dresser (furniture)	une commode
to drink	boire
to drive	conduire, rouler
driver	un conducteur
drugstore	la droguerie
dry cleaner	la teinturerie
dubbed	doublé

duty-free	une boutique hors taxes
E	
ear	une oreille
early	en avance
to earn	gagner
earring	une boucle d'oreille
east	est
to eat	manger
economy car	une voiture économie
economy class	la classe touriste
egg	l'oeuf (m)
elbow	le coude
electrician	un électricien
elevator	un ascenseur
eleven	onze
e-mail	le courriel
embarassed	confus/confuse
Emergency!	Urgence°
employee	un(e) employé(e)
engineer	un ingénieur
to enhance	mettre en relief
enjoy your meal	bon appétit !
envelope	une enveloppe
eraser	une gomme
espresso	un express
exchange rate	le taux de change
excuse me	excusez-moi
explosion	une explosion
Express mail	Chronopost
eye(s)	un oeil (des yeux)
F	
face	le visage
to face up to	faire face à
to faint	s'évanouir

far (from)	loin (de)
farewell	adieu
fat	gros/grosse
father	un père
fees	les frais (m)
to fetch, get	aller chercher
fever	la fièvre
fiancé(e)	un(e) fiancé(e)
to fill up	faire le plein
filling	un plombage
fine	ça va
finger	le doigt
fire	un feu
Fire!	Au feu !
to fire (someone)	renvoyer (quelqu'un)
fireman	un pompier
first class	la première classe
first floor (US), ground floor	le rez-de-chaussée
fish	le poisson
to fish	pêcher
fishing	la pêche
flight	un vol
flight attendant	un steward, une hôtesse de l'air
flood	une inondation
floor	le sol
flowers	des fleurs
flu	la grippe
foggy	du brouillard
foot	un pied
football	le football américain
for	pour
fork	une fourchette
freeze	geler
friend	un(e) ami(e)

friendly	amical
fries	les frites
fruit	les fruits
frying pan	une poêle
funny	drôle

G

garden, yard	le jardin
to garden	jardiner, faire du jardinage
gas, petrol	de l'essence (f)
gas station	une station-service
gate	une porte (aéroport)
general delivery	la poste restante
girl	une fille
girlfriend	une copine
to give	donner
to give a reason	rendre raison
to give up	donner sa langue au chat
to give thanks to	rendre grâce à
glass	un verre
glasses	des lunettes
to glorify	rendre gloire à
gloves	des gants
to go	aller
Go ahead!	Allez-y !
good	bon/bonne
Good evening	Bonsoir
Good night	Bonne nuit
Good-bye	Au revoir
grape	un raisin
grapefruit	un pamplemousse
gray	gris/grise
green	vert/verte
grocery store	l'épicerie (f)
guitar	la guitare

gums	la gencive
gunshot	un coup de feu

H

hair	les cheveux
hairdresser	le coiffeur
half slip	un jupon
hall	le couloir
hand	la main
handkerchief	un mouchoir
handsome	beau
to hang up	raccrocher
happy	heureux/ heureuse
hard-working	travailleur
hat	un chapeau
to have	avoir
head	la tête
headache	mal à la tête
headlights	les phares (m)
heartburn	des brûlures d'estomac
heavy	lourd/lourde
Hello	Bonjour
Hello? (on the phone)	Allô?
help	de l'assistance (f)
Help!	Au secours!
Hi	Salut
high beams	les feux de route
high school	un lycée
highway	une autoroute
to hike	faire de la randonnée
hiking	la randonnée
to hire	embaucher
hold mail	la poste restante
homework	des devoirs
honeymoon	la lune de miel

hospital	l'hôpital (m)
hot	chaud/chaude
hotel	un hôtel
hotel room	une chambre
house	la maison
how	comment
How are you?	Ça va?
How much is it?	C'est combien?
humid	humide
to hunt	(aller) chasser
to hunt for	faire la chasse à
hunting	la chasse
to hurt	avoir mal, faire mal à
husband	un mari, un époux
hyper(active)	excité/excitée

I

ice cream	la glace
immigration	l'immigration (f)
impatient	impatient/impatiente
in a hurry	pressé/pressée
in back of	en arrière de
in economy class	en classe touriste
in first class	en première classe
in front of	en avant de
inbox	le courrier arrivé
inch	un pouce
infected	infecté/infectée
injection	une piqûre
insomnia	insomniaque
insured	assuré/assurée
to intend to	avoir l'intention de
interest rate	le taux d'intérêt

J, K

jacket	un blouson

jam	la confiture
jar, cup	un pot
jewelry	des bijoux
jogging	le jogging
juice	le jus
to kick	donner un coup de pied
kilogram	un kilogramme de
kind	gentil/gentille
kitchen	la cuisine
knee	le genou
knife	un couteau

L

lamb	l'agneau
to land	atterrir
lamp	une lampe
late	en retard
laundromat	la blanchisserie
laundry service	le service de blanchisserie
lawyer, barrister	un(e) avocat(e)
to lay off	licencier
lazy	paresseux/paresseuse
to leave a message	laisser un message
left	(à) gauche
leg	la jambe
lemon	un citron
lemonade	le citron pressé
Let's go!	Allons-y !
letter	une lettre
lip	la lèvre
lipstick	le rouge à lèvres
to listen to music	écouter (de) la musique
liter	un litre
living room	le salon
loan	un emprunt

local anesthesia	une anesthésie locale
lonely	solitaire
long	long
to lose	perdre
lover	un(e) amant(e)
lunch	le déjeuner
luxury car	une voiture luxe

M

Ma'am, Mrs.	Madame
magazine	un magazine
maid	une femme de chambre
mail	le courrier
mailbox	une boîte aux lettres
main course	le plat principal
to make, do	faire
to make the bed	faire le lit
makeup (cosmetic)	le maquillage
makeup remover	le démaquillant
man	un homme
manager	un gérant, un responsable
map	une carte
marriage	le mariage
to marry	s'épouser
mayonnaise	la mayonnaise
meal	le repas
mean	méchant/méchante
measuring cup	un verre gradué
measuring spoon	une cuiller à mesurer
mechanic	un mécanicien
medium-rare	à point
to meet	faire la connaissance de
menu	la carte
microwave	un four à micro-ondes
midnight	minuit

mid-size car	une voiture intermédiaire
mile (1.6 km)	un mille
milk	le lait
million	un million
mirror	un miroir
Miss	Mademoiselle
mistake	une erreur
moisturizer	la crème hydratante
money	de l'argent (m)
money exchange	le bureau de change
money order	le mandat
moped	une mobylette
more, very	plus
mother	une mèr
motorbike	une moto
mouth	la bouche
movie	le film
movie theater	le cinéma
Mr.	Monsieur
Mrs., Ma'am	Madame
muffler	un cache-nez
museum	le musée
music	la musique
mustard	la moutarde

N

naive	naïf/naïve
napkin	une serviette
near (to)	près (de)
necessary	nécessaire
neck	le cou
necklace	un collier
to need	avoir besoin de
nephew	un neveu
nervous	nerveux/nerveuse

newspaper	un journal
newsstand	un kiosque
next to	à côté de
nice	sympathique (or sympa)
nice (weather)	beau
niece	une nièce
nightgown	une chemise de nuit
no	non
noon	midi
north	nord
nose	le nez
note, bill, paper money	un billet
notebook	un cahier
nothing	rien
Novocaln	la Novocaïnc
nurse	un infirmier/une infirmièr

O

obvious	évident
office	un bureau
OK	d'accord
on the way	en route
one	un, une
onion	un oignon
to open	ouvrir
open-minded	sans préjugés
opera	l'opéra (m)
or	ou
orange	une orange
orange (color)	l'orange (f)
orchestra	l'orchestre (m)
to order	commander
other	autre
outbox	le courrier départ
outdoor market	le marché

outgoing	ouvert/ouverte
oven	un four
oven mitt	un gant de cuisine
to pack	faire les bagages, valises

P, Q

package	un colis, un paquet
painting	une peinture
pajamas	un pyjama
pants	un pantalon
paper	le papier
paper clip	un trombone
paper money, note, bill	un billet
pardon me	pardon
park	le parc
to park	stationner
to pass	doubler
passenger	un passager
passport	un passeport
pasta	les pâtes
pastry shop	la pâtisserie
patient	patient/patiente
patio	le patio
patriotic	patriotique
to pay	payer
to pay a visit	faire une visite, rendre visite à
to pay attention to	faire attention à
to pay for	mettre de l'argent pour
to pay the bill	régler le compte
peach	une pêche
peanut	l'arachide, la cacahuète
pear	une poire
peas	petits pois (m)
pets	les animaux
pharmacist	un(e) pharmacien(ne)

pharmacy	la pharmacie
phone book	un annuaire
phone booth	une cabine téléphonique
phone number	un numéro de téléphone
piano	le piano
to pick up (the phone)	décrocher
pie	la tarte
pillow	un oreiller
pilot	le pilote
pin	une épingle
pink	rose
plane ticket	le billet d'avion
plans	des projets (m)
plate	une assiette
platform	le quai
to play music	jouer de la musique
playful	taquin/taquine
please	s'il vous / te plaît
Please hold	Ne quittez pas
police officer	un policier
police station	le commissariat
pool	la piscine
porch	le porche
pork	le porc
post card	une carte postale
post office	la poste, les P.T.T.
pot	une marmite
potato	la pomme de terre
pound (weight)	une livre
pregnant	enceinte
present	un cadeau
to pretend to	faire semblant de
pretty	belle, jolie
price	le prix

printer	une imprimante
problem	problème
to pull out, remove	arracher
purple	violet
purse	un sac à main
to put money into	mettre de l'argent dans
to put on make-up	se maquiller
quarter	le quart

R

rabbit	le lapin
rare (meat)	bleu
razor	le rasoir
to read	lire
reading	la lecture
receipt	un reçu
receptionist	un(e) réceptionniste
recipe	une recette
recipient	le destinataire
red	rouge
red (hair)	roux
refrigerator	un réfrigérateur
registered	recommandé/recommandée
regular gas	essence ordinaire
to repeat	répéter
to replace	remplacer
reservation	une réservation
restaurant	le restaurant
return receipt	l'avis de réception
ribbon	un ruban
rice	le riz
to ride in a car	aller en voiture
right (direction)	(à) droit(e)
ring	une bague
to ring	sonner

to rinse	rincer
room	la pièce, la salle
round trip ticket	un billet aller-retour
rug	un tapis
to run errands	faire les courses
rushed	pressé/pressée
Russian	russe
rye bread	le pain de seigle

S

sad	triste
sailing	la voile
salad	la salade
salt	le sel
sandals	des sandales
saucer	une soucoupe
to save money, save up	faire des économies
savings account	un compte d'épargne
to say good-bye	faire ses adieux
scared	effrayé/effrayée
scarf	un foulard
school	une école
seasons	les saisons (f)
seat	la place
second floor (US)	le premier étage
secretary	un(e) secrétaire
see you soon	à bientôt
see you tomorrow	à demain
to sell	vendre
sender	l'expéditeur (m)
serious	sérieux/sérieuse
to set the alarm	mettre le réveil
to set the table	mettre la table
Shall we go?	On y va?
shampoo	le shampooing

to shave	se raser
shaver	le rasoir électrique
shaving	le rasage
she	elle
shelf	une étagère
shirt	une chemise
shoes	des chaussures
short (height)	petit/petite
short (length)	court/courte
shorts	un short
shoulder	une épaule
show, performance	un spectacle
shower	la douche
showing, time	la séance
shy	timide
sick	malade
to sign	signer
Sir	Monsieur
sister	une soeur
size	la dimension, la taille
skating	le patinage
to ski	skier, faire du ski
skiing	le ski
skirt	une jupe
slowly	lentement
smart	intelligent/intelligente
smoke	fumer
snack	le goûter
snails	les escargots
sneakers	des tennis
to sneeze	éternuer
snobbish	snob
to snow	neiger
soap	le savon

soccer	le football, le foot
socks	des chaussettes
sofa	le canapé
son	un fils
sophisticated	raffiné/raffinée
sorry, distressed	navré/navrée
so-so	comme ci, comme ça
south	sud
special delivery	par express
to spend	dépenser
to spend money	dépenser
spoon	une cuiller
sport jacket	une veste de sport
spring	printemps (m)
stamp	un timbre
staple	une agrafe
steak	le bifteck
steering wheel	le volant
stereo	une chaîne stéréo
stockings	des bas
stomach	un estomac
stop light	le feu rouge
stopover	une escale
stores	les magasins
stormy	orageux/orageuse
stove	une cuisinière
straight (hair)	raide
straight ahead	tout droit
street	la rue
strong	fort/forte
student	un(e) étudiant(e)
studious	studieux/studieuse
study (room)	un bureau
stupid	stupide

subtitled	sous-titré
subway	le métro
subway station	la gare/station de métro
sugar	le sucre
to sulk	faire la tête
sum, amount, total	le montant
summer	l'été (m)
sunny	du soleil
sure	sûr
sweater	un pull
to swim	nager
swimming	la natation
symphony	la symphonie

T

table	une table
tablespoon	une cuillère à soupe
tall	grand/grande
to take a trip	faire un voyage
to take off	décoller
tanned	bronzé/bronzée
taxi stand	la station de taxi
tea	le thé
teacher	un professeur, un(e) enseignant(e)
telephone	un téléphone
television	la télévision
temporary	provisoire
tennis	le tennis
terminal	une aérogare
test	un examen
thank you (very much)	merci (bien/beaucoup)
theater	le théâtre
theft	le vol
Thief!	Au voleur!
thin	mince

thing	chose
to think	penser
thousand	mille
to throw up	vomir
thumb	le pouce
tie	une cravate
tie pin	une épingle de cravate
tights	un collant
time	le temps
tip	le pourboire
tip included	service compris
tired	fatigué/fatiguée
toast	le pain grillé
toaster	un grille-pain
tobacco store	un tabac
toe	un orteil
toilet	la toilette, les W.-C., les toilettes
total, amount, sum	le montant
towel	la serviette
traffic jam	un embouteillage
train	le train
train station	la gare
transportation	le transport
traveler's check	un chèque de voyage
trip	une excursion
truck	un camion
true	vrai/vraie
T-shirt	un tee-shirt
to turn	tourner
to turn on the radio,	mettre la radio, les informations
tuxedo	un smoking
TV	la télé
tweezers	la pince à épiler
typewriter	une machine à écrire

U, V

ugly	moche, laid
umbrella	un parapluie
uncle	un oncle
undershirt	un maillot de corps
underwear	un sous-vêtement
unfriendly	froid/froide
unleavened bread	le pain azyme
unlikely	peu probable
until next time	à la prochaine
up	en haut
useful	utile
useless	inutile
vegetarian	végétarien(ne)
visa	un visa
to visit someone	rendre visite à quelqu'un

W, Y

waiter	un serveur
waitress	une serveuse
walk	promenade
wall	un mur
wallet	un portefeuille
to want	avoir envie de, vouloir
to wash	se laver
to wash the dishes	faire la vaisselle
watch	une montre
to watch a movie	regarder un film
to watch out for	faire attention à
Watch out!	Attention !
water	l'eau (f)
water skiing	le ski nautique
wavy	ondulé/ondulée
weak	faible
wedding	les noces, le mariage

weight	le poids
to welcome	faire bon accueil
well done (meat)	bien cuit
west	ouest
what	quoi
What?	Comment?
wheat	le blé
when	quand
where	où
Where is . . . ?	Où est . . . ?
white	blanc/blanche
who	qui
why	pourquoi
wife	une femme, une épouse
wine	le vin
woman	une femme
to work	travailler
worried	inquiet/inquiete
to worship	rendre un culte à
to wrestle	lutter
wrestling	la lutte
wrist	le poignet
to write	écrire
writer	un écrivain
yes	oui
you're welcome	de rien

Index